1999

THE

TRUST

FACTOR

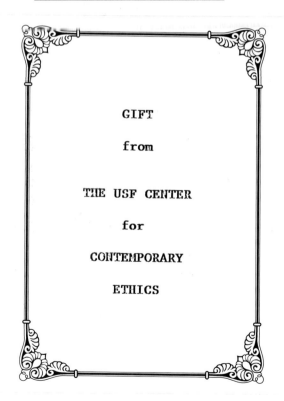

GIFT

from

THE USF CENTER

for

CONTEMPORARY

ETHICS

THE

TRUST

FACTOR

The Art of Doing Business
in the 21st Century

Cheryl A. Chatfield, Ph.D.

UNIVERSITY
PRESS
SANTA FE

Sunstone books may be purchased for educational, business, or sales promotional use. For information please write: Special Markets Department, Sunstone Press, P.O. Box 2321, Santa Fe, New Mexico 87504-2321.

FIRST EDITION

10 9 8 7 6 5 4 3 2 1

Library of Congress Cataloging in Publication Data:
Chatfield, Cheryl A., 1946–
    The trust factor: the art of doing business in the 21st century / Cheryl A. Chatfield.
       p. cm.
    includes index.
    ISBN: 0-86534-264-4
    1. Business ethics. 2. Trust (Psychology) I. Title.
HF 5387 . C453   1997
174' .4—dc21   97-21295
                                CIP

Published by   SUNSTONE PRESS
                      Post Office Box 2321
                      Santa Fe, NM 87504-2321 / USA
                      (505) 988-4418 / *orders only* (800) 243-5644
                      FAX (505) 988-1025

ACKNOWLEDGMENTS

Many thanks

    to Sare Orsdell who helped with editing and inspiration
    to my sister, Mary Chatfield Jones, who helped in every way
    to Pamela Massa who helped with encouragement
    to Donna Domizio who helped by being my friend

                          I love you all

CONTENTS

PART II
DEFINING TRUST IN THE WORKPLACE

PART III
IMPLEMENTING TRUST IN THE WORKPLACE

LIST OF EXERCISES

INTRODUCTION

In 1993, I stood in court as the judge pronounced me guilty of a felony charge and sentenced me to 200 hours of community service, 5 years of probation to repay $25,000 and one night in jail.

I started out as a high school English teacher from a conservative New England family of a college administrator father and social worker mother. I earned a doctorate in education, taught at the college level and then left education for the better rewards and excitement of the stock brokerage industry. What happened? Even four years later, I don't have all the answers. But my arrest and conviction forced me to look at my life and reassess the business world around me. My story serves as an illustration of what must change in order for businesses to survive in the next century.

We are in a transitional age, a time of change. We recognize that business can no longer be done as it has been in the past. Market conditions are rapidly fluctuating and much of our time is spent on keeping up with the daily crises. There is little energy left at the end of the day to plan for next year, next week, or even tomorrow. We are trying to balance family with work and live up to that "quality of life" we always hear about. Employee concerns seem constant and some days we have no patience for the endless questions that must be addressed. Other days we wonder if we will be able to avoid the temptation of questionable business practices in order to maintain our profit. It is difficult to feel happy with our current successes and there is that recurring thought that "something is missing."

Despite our determination to the contrary, we feel that we can no longer rely on the integrity of others. We have lost faith in our own intuition and often listen to outside sources rather than trust our instincts. We no longer feel secure that the future will work out for the best and we are not quite sure how to prepare for that. An accumulation of these thoughts often permeates our daily interactions and leaves us with a vague sense of loss. We want to continue with our old optimism but many events seem to contradict our belief in that process.

How do we manage the change, the ethics, the people, the profit and the unrest? What is the common thread that unites them all? How do we get back a sense of control? How can we regain a sense of security? How can we begin to rely again on our own decisions and how can we reestablish a faith in the others around us?

This book suggests that there is an underlying theme of lack of trust in our businesses and in our lives. This distrust has reached significant proportions and is the key to the challenges and changes we face in order to successfully enter the 21st century.

Business is built on trust. But just as it is an acknowledged component in business, it is obviously a missing component. Outright lying has become commonplace at many companies and some managers even admit writing deceptive internal reports. But it is not only employees that are viewed as deceitful; leaders are equally viewed as untrustworthy. The public does not rate business executives as pillars of ethical behavior. Economics seems to have become separated from ethics and human values. Entrepreneurial students in my business class at the University of New Mexico in 1996 were very clear about what was right or wrong in relation to business practices. But they also indicated that in business one must make whatever decisions are necessary, even if those decisions are unethical ones. This is how workers, the public, and our youth entering the workplace view business. It is not about doing business with integrity. It is about making expedient decisions, even very clear unethical ones, such as lying and deception to customer, employer, and employee.

This apparent lack of trust is just as prevalent in other segments of our society. Studies show that the 1990s are characterized by a deteriorating lack of faith in the government, the media, public education, and doctors, as well as corporations. Business is not the only culprit; it is just the main focus of this book. Lack of business integrity has been evident for decades. It was really part of the 1960s rebellious cries. Government, big business, and institutions were not meeting the needs of individuals and were being deceptive. To the baby boomers, those born between 1946 and 1964, this is old news—news that was rejected in the process of growing up when it became clear that to fight the system was too difficult. So most baby boomers chose to work in the very industries that they or their contemporaries protested decades earlier. What is different now?

One answer is that the lack of trust is both more obvious and more widespread. It is not just the external dealings that are suspicious. The questioning has expanded internally. The 1960s was about distrust of politics and large organizations. Things got worse in the 1970s after Vietnam and Watergate. These and other events seemed to precipitate an insidious infiltration of our thoughts. We knew what was right and wrong, but we just switched our conscience to "off" or "standby" and became increasingly numb to our surroundings and the consequences of our actions. The distrust affected our ability to act correctly, to provide a secure future, and to interact effectively with others.

The good news is that the times are changing. The lack of integrity in our lives has gotten far enough out of hand to capture our attention and force us to reengage our conscience and recognize the need to be responsible for our actions. Part I presents three very specific reasons for optimism: 1) We are now in the information age with its new demands; 2) we are in the midst of newly discovered scientific theories that give us a different view of the world; and 3) we are in a time when the baby boomers who were the young protesters of the 1960s are now the business leaders asking some of the same questions. People such as myself have experienced the downfalls of doing business the old way. This book suggests that we can begin to trust again because it is economically feasible, scientifically possible, and philosophically and socially acceptable to do so.

Part II defines trust in the workplace and provides answers about what we can do. Basically, we need to begin to trust again. But "trusting again" has become an empty concept as our experiences have, in some cases, justifiably jaded our view of others. There must be a process whereby we can gradually feel it is safe to venture out of our isolation and skepticism. The first step is to relearn to trust ourselves. Self esteem, an over-used term of the 1990s, must no longer be equated with money in business.

Learning to trust others is the second step. This includes accepting the racial, ethnic, gender and sexual preference diversity that still seems to plague us. The third step is establishing an external ethical standard. Much research has been done in the area of ethical theories, but the fact remains that there are some simple rules, such as no lying, no cheating, and no stealing, that have been forgotten. Spirituality has been ignored too long within our business environment. But we need to redefine this spirituality and view it separately from religion. The emphasis here is on values, not religious beliefs.

Part III presents practical methods of implementing trust into the workplace on a daily basis. Six specific exercises are provided to assess yourself and your company in relation to trust. The exercises address the entrepreneurial thinking of change and adaptability. No business will survive or be successful without being able to easily adapt to, even if not be comfortable with, change.

Interdependence must be encouraged. In the process of learning to trust again, we need training on how to function within teams. If we accept that changes are occurring more rapidly and we expect ourselves and our employees to be able to meet the challenges, what about the thinking process necessary to do so? Specific tasks are suggested for hiring, training, insisting on accountability, and providing new types of rewards.

Some chapters include a section entitled "My Story" that presents the chronological events leading up to my day in court. My experiences are used to remind us that we have left the human element out of business for too long. We must bring individuals back into the picture.

In any change there must be balance between the old and the new. This book does not suggest replacing the bottom line with concern for the individual. It is necessary to incorporate both, not exclude either. The concept of balance is an evolutionary step for our society. There has not been much evidence of it during the extremes of the industrial age. So far, the beginnings of the information age exhibit the same excessive beliefs in an all-encompassing answer. We now have the chance to use our technology for the good of humankind, trusting ourselves more than our machines. Moderation seems to be one of our greatest challenges in shaping this time of transition.

The Conclusion provides a tool, "What is Your Trust Factor?" to measure individual integrity and that of companies. This tool will help determine where one stands on the issue of trust in business and what can be done about it. We are entering a new era, one in which maintenance of the status quo is no longer a viable option. It is time to do something about redirecting our turbulent times. In the 1960s, the talk of values fell on deaf ears because there was no external justification for it. Now, technology, science and public opinion have created an opening in our economic structure to institute some of those changes that were defined decades ago. This book poses the challenge of trusting again, provides the pragmatic ways of acting on our beliefs, and ponders the task of making a difference in our economic future.

PART I

REINTRODUCING
TRUST INTO BUSINESS

Reintroducing trust into business requires reverting back to the human element. Business is about people, not just products. The sections throughout the book entitled, " My Story," show the human element. No story serves as an exact example. No story is that simple. My experiences are important in that they are real. I did some wrong things. I got caught. I paid a price. This book grew out of my lessons. I can only speak about that which I gained from first-hand knowledge. I now know the importance of trusting myself and my beliefs, and not being influenced by external pressures to be someone lesser than I am.

I am a product of my environment and the times, not a victim of them. My life reflects the excesses of the industrial era. I was forced to change as a result of bad choices. Trust had become a complex issue, reflecting difficult times. I learned to extradite the simplicity and restore trust into my life. I hope my narrative will help others do the same.

With my story as the backdrop, Chapters 1-3 present the changes we face as we move from the industrial era to a computer-driven time with its accessible knowledge. Economics, science and philosophy provide insight into the new era.

1

ECONOMIC FEASIBILITY

THE NEW ERA

Is it to be called the information age, the knowledge age or some yet to be determined name? Whatever the outcome, one thing is certain—we are no longer in the industrial era. Computers have led us to a new time. We are in a transition that is still being defined. Peter Drucker, in *Post-Capitalist Society,* claims that this transformation already "has changed the political, economic, social, and moral landscape of the world."[1] Alvin and Heidi Toffler, in *Creating A New Civilization: The Politics of the Third Wave,* agree that this new age "implies, in short, a true transformation in human affairs."[2]

How many of us are prepared to face a major change in all aspects of our lives? If we choose to face reality, we begin to understand that we can no longer live and work the way we are currently doing. Not everyone will face events as drastic as those that forced me to transform my life. Not everyone needs to make an extreme external change. Yet we all need to look at our beliefs and recognize the necessity of some shift.

MY STORY— THE BEGINNING

Moving to Santa Fe in 1987 was a dream come true. I had fallen in love with the city the first time I had visited there in 1980. Santa Fe is called the City Different because it is so unusual. The adobe-style architecture, the narrow streets, the quaint shops, and the strong Native American and Hispanic influence combine with an energy to create a place where people feel "different." Most can't explain why, they just like to visit the city. I know I always felt better there.

I was running a small stock brokerage firm that I had started years earlier in Denver. It was a firm that specialized in low-priced or "penny stocks," so called because some of the stocks sold for as little as $.01 a share. After years of being a high school English teacher, a public school administrator and then a college instructor, I had become enthralled with the stock market in Denver. It took me a year before I understood that a person from a family of teachers and social workers could leave the world of service and enter the capitalistic work of a stock broker. I felt I was providing a service in helping people with their financial future. I spent much time doing seminars and educating people to the market.

Once in Santa Fe I decided to begin expanding my brokerage firm by hiring brokers, moving into a bigger space, setting up a second corporation to fund venture projects, and then setting up satellite offices in Denver and Cheyenne, Wyoming. I wish I could look back and feel good about that growth. The business decisions on one level were very appropriate and wise, and the people I hired were, for the most part, very capable. Yet it was the beginning of a destructive pattern. I was living on borrowed money. I never really had the funds to expand the business. There were past debts, many from a divorce, that never got paid because I never got ahead. It wasn't poor planning as much as being an eternal optimist and expecting money to always be there if I worked hard. This was a belief that others may also have, assuming that things would always get better and not being prepared in case they got worse.

In the industry of the penny stock market, it was initially easy to make good money. In the 80s, the market was wild with stock prices increasing 2-10 times within 3 weeks or less and brokers making $5,000-10,000 a week or more. Brokers lived a fast paced life-style. My extravagance was owning a private airplane and such things as giving my husband a surprise birthday present of a weekend at the Plaza Hotel in New York City—we were living in Denver. Money flowed freely and we assumed it would never end.

But it did end. By the mid 80s, there were major problems in the Over the Counter, or OTC, market. Government regulators were cracking down on the abuses and, of course, with so much money being made, there were abuses. But even more significantly, investors were no longer buying as freely as they had been. The reasons were simple. The returns on the low-priced stocks were no longer worth the risk. Over the years, investors watched these small publicly-traded companies go up in price and then in a year or two run out of money and go out of business or simply languish with no corporate or stock activity. This was a matter of our financial system at work. Investors will buy when stocks are increasing in value and making money. When prices decline and investors lose money, people do not buy. I observed how government often tries to over-regulate. Certainly there were abuses in the market that should not have occurred and many investors lost money. But by the time the regulators acted, the damage was done.

By the mid 80s, many investors realized there was too much risk for the potential rewards and they stopped investing as the companies stopped performing. Our financial system has its own inherent safeguards built in. Investors are always looking for a better return and if the profit potential is there, they are willing to take the risk. In the low-priced stocks, the risk was that the companies were unproven. In many instances, they were brand new companies with no track record. At the height of the penny market, it was oil and gas exploration that enticed everyone. Companies would start up, go public, raise a million or more dollars, and then try to compete in the very speculative oil and gas arena. Many companies had management with little or no experience. I remember one that had a dentist as president. Needless to say, most of these companies ran out of money long before they succeeded drilling successful wells. Things got worse when the oil price declined. It was no longer profitable for a small company to compete. A similar scenario, although less dramatic, played out for small publicly traded companies in other industries. It is easy to look back now and realize that companies should not go public with limited experience and limited funds. At the time, however, I was still caught in the belief that even though the frenzy of the market had quieted, there were still legitimate companies deserving to go public or have private funds raised for them. I was then, and still am, a firm believer in the future of small companies being the backbone of our country's success. But the process of providing money to these companies needed a serious review.

My indictment of the penny stock market and its abuses is not an indictment of the overall stock market. Buying stocks and bonds has always been one of the best investments. Penny stocks, once so prominent in such centers as Denver, New York, and Spokane in the 80s, are rarely traded today. Even at the height of the penny market, brokers at a large firm such as Merrill Lynch would rarely buy these low-priced stocks for their clients. There were two different worlds, both dealing with stocks, but one concentrating on the much more speculative arena.

My actions of living on borrowed money continued. I kept my business going and kept expanding. By January 1989, I realized that things were not going as well as expected. I had the opportunity to join forces with a partner who brought money and the experience of running a large brokerage firm to the table. In retrospect, it was the beginning of the end and may have been the single worst decision of my life.

I moved back to Denver, closed the Santa Fe office, and began another new life. This was the beginning of a most exciting business time as well as a most frustrating one. Any attempt to describe my new business partner would be less than complete. He was one of the brightest, funniest, most likable, most effective, as well as most infuriating people I have ever known. I enjoyed working with him because he was so quick. We worked hard, enjoyed it, and laughed a lot in the process. We worked long 15-hour days and then would spend at least an hour talking on the phone at night. We built the brokerage firm from a few brokers to over 100 employees. Anyone who has ever set up her or his own business knows the thrill of the first year when all energy is strictly focused on one goal—getting the business successful. I used to say that the business was my life. At the time, it was.

As the first year progressed, it became clear that my goals and those of my partner were quite different. I became frustrated that as we began to make money at the firm, greed seemed to be taking over. My partner was frustrated that I was more worried about investors' needs and integrity than about profit. We both had a point.

By March 1990, I felt I could not continue. I spent many hours agonizing over a fateful decision. I knew something needed to be done. I felt my partner might listen because, despite our differences, we respected one another and we had become friends. So one March morning, I sat down with him privately and confronted him with the fact that the partnership wasn't working.

I did not want a corporate struggle. No one really wins. If my partner was unwilling to listen to my concerns, there really was no future for our partnership anyway. He didn't listen and maneuvered to get the one minority shareholder to vote with him to fire me as CEO and have me leave the firm. We negotiated an agreement and he bought me out. He probably will never understand that I did what I had to do, not out of betrayal or naiveté, but out of respect and integrity, fully aware of the consequences. I am not sorry about the outcome. I am sorry about the loss of what could have been a great OTC stock brokerage firm. However, by the time I left, the firm no longer represented my values.

I lost a job and a corporation. I needed to decide what to do next. Within a week, I purchased another firm. Within a month I had new offices and employees, with others waiting to be hired. I'm not sure making such a quick decision was wise. But it seemed like the only viable plan at the time. After 10 years in the stock brokerage industry, I felt it was all I wanted to, or could do. I loved the business.

The new firm was going to be different. I had no use for the macho-dominated, greed-focused, unethical practices I had encountered. I knew there was a better way. I knew women had a different approach to business and I wanted to try to establish a firm that represented all the values that were important to me. So I named the firm *Women Securities International* with the intent of focusing, although not exclusively, on assisting women with financial advice. My initial employees had been with me at the previous firm. They knew they could no longer work with my former partner and were willing to take a risk with me. The beginning, as always, was exciting. We created not just a business, but a vision. We were not just going to sell stocks. We were going to help people prepare for their future by investing in socially responsible stocks. We were also going to raise money for small companies that were socially conscious.

This new firm never achieved financial success; but in looking back, it did achieve a moral victory. Again, I was guilty of optimism. At the time I had no reason to believe otherwise. I saw the new firm as the opportunity to run a business based on all of the ideals I was unable to execute at my previous firm. Our vision was a little ahead of its time. Even though we got tremendous responses at the seminars, most women weren't quite prepared to make the commitment to enact the plans. Wanting to help women was a good decision, however. It even surprised me that the name of our firm and our focus did not keep away the male brokers that I wanted to hire.

A fallacy in the plan was not enough money. This was one of the reasons for the downfall. The other reason was sabotage activities unknown to me at the time. But that part of the story will be told later.

NEW ERA TRANSITION

Remember that the world is in transition. It is not unusual to feel unrest in a time of change. History shows that the shift from the agricultural to the industrial age was a turbulent one with external destruction. Today the changes seem to be more internal, but no less extreme. My own story illustrates some of these points.

While transitions can be difficult, there is another view. Even though there will be unrest, there is also the opportunity to help shape the new. This is the approach suggested here. To sit back and passively view the turmoil without taking some initiatives is inexcusable. A new era brings potentially positive events. Changes in the past led to an improved lifestyle and were a leap forward. Do not get bogged down in the mire of this shift and forget the necessary process towards a better future. We can help shape the new millennium by better understanding our current situation.

ECONOMIC FEASIBILITY OF TRUST

In order for trust to be incorporated into business, it must be economically feasible to do so. This is a cold, hard fact about business. Too often we try to argue other functions of our corporations; however, the main goal is profit. Profit assures survival and thus potential success. It must be pointed out that "profit" as used here does not refer to the excessive greed that dominates some businesses. There is nothing wrong with profit. It is only in the extreme that it becomes indefensible. I participated in a business where greed dominated. I saw the repercussions to this type of thinking. But I also learned that I was naive to promote trust and integrity in an environment that only valued profit. Today, our overall business climate is beginning to change.

During the industrial era, which has dominated our business consciousness until recently, trust became an unnecessary commodity. With the information age comes a new potential. The computer is helping to create a workplace in which trust can not only survive but thrive. The information age is opening up the opportunity of an economy of abundance and a people-centered work environment.

Abundance

First, it is important to understand that the traditional and historical basis of our economic system is one of scarcity. An economic system is the way a society manages the production, distribution, and consumption of its wealth. The major factors of production are land, labor, and capital. The dominant thinking has been that these resources are scarce, in the sense that there is only a limited amount of each available. But the information age challenges us to redefine these resources.

Peter Drucker explains, "the real controlling resources and the absolutely decisive 'factor of production' is now neither capital nor land nor labor. It is knowledge."[3] The whole basis of our economic system has changed as a result of the computer providing access to seemingly unlimited knowledge. This knowledge can provide access to other resources since the computer can provide information to everyone about land, labor, and capital. But this idea of abundance replacing scarcity must be understood. New concepts are not easily assimilated into our thought process because we tend to resist change. The implications of this change are far-reaching. Think about how the concept of "enough for all" will radically alter much in our current business strategy. If we really believed that there would be enough of the right people, enough money, and enough space to do business, we might function in a very different manner.

Another aspect of abundance impacted by the computer is the capacity of the computer chip. This has been increasing while its energy consumption remains relatively low. We are able to do more with less. These two ideas of unlimited resources and doing more with less affect our whole economic system. But it takes time for new ideas to permeate our thinking and then affect our actions.

Skilled Workers

Another benefit to the information age is the fact that it has created an opportunity for people to be important again. In the industrial era, the individual worker became less significant because people could easily be trained to replace one another on the assembly line. That mentality dominated the middle part of this century. But now, with the computers requiring more trained expertise, it is not as easy to replace one operator with another. When workers leave a business, they often take important skills, such as the intricacies of a particular software, with them. This knowledge is not easily replaced.

Few owners or workers understand all facets of their business as they did in the past. Advanced software is too extensive, too complicated, and too changing for management to understand all the tasks and nuances involved. Every industry has so much new technology and software that one manager or owner cannot possibly keep up with all the innovations, forcing reliance more and more on the workers. If handled correctly, everyone can win in this new scenario.

As part of understanding this age of change, workers must also be prepared to have their jobs become obsolete. Accepting this situation puts the worker in a position of constantly being abreast of current changes within an industry. It is foolish to think of this as unfair. It simply is the way that it is. These technological changes create the need for highly skilled employees. The worker becomes increasingly more important.

Downsizing

The information age has also brought downsizing. Facing this very real threat, people are no longer the old "company-workers" who expect to stay with the same corporation for their whole life and to be taken care of by that corporation. Those days are gone and with them goes loyalty. Organizations need to understand this. This puts responsibility on both parties. Companies need to recognize their role in earning the trust of their employees as is evidenced by the recent emphasis on regaining employee loyalty.

In October of 1996, I was invited to speak at a meeting of the Human Resource Association of Central Connecticut. A poll of their members, representing large and small companies in the state, indicated that one of their most important concerns was employee loyalty. How can a worker today be loyal to and trust any organization that is downsizing? It was interesting that even in this group of top human resource managers, many felt sympathetic to the problem of loyalty since they were facing loss of their jobs and they realized how angry they felt about that prospect. People question why they should feel loyalty while continually facing potential loss of their jobs. Others talk of their feelings of dependency and their fears in a time when they see the layoffs strictly in terms of economics, with no regard for the individual. These workers feel devalued, with their previous allegiance not being rewarded.

The changes are happening. Corporations can either be a

part of these changes and encourage them, or be left behind. Workers are recognizing that they will no longer be taken care of and thus no longer need to be subservient to the organization. Employees need to recognize that they must accept a certain instability and prepare their lives according. This means knowing and trusting one's own strengths and the strengths of the company.

Technology is the driving force behind the changes. Computers can now do the work faster and cheaper than employees. Despite the high costs to implement the new technology, businesses are compelled to keep abreast of the latest developments in order to compete effectively in a global market. There is little choice for the corporations. It is unfair to blame them for this turnaround. Often greed does take control. But the reality is that new technology brings a replacement of certain workers.

New Developments

As we know and as we see in our daily lives, many people are not feeling good about the future. It may be difficult to define exactly, but there is a feeling of apprehension. I have listened to TV programs in which panelists try to negate these feelings. After all, the Dow is at an all-time high, the economy seems robust . . . and the story goes on. But the reality is that even though personal income of Americans has increased significantly since 1983, 98% of the increase went to the top 20 percent of the workers.

In the 1950s to the 1970s, you could 'buy' a good education, safe streets, and a safe neighborhood, a good job, an increasing standard of living. That was the American promise, and that promise was actually delivered. People came to expect it, and this wasn't unrealistic at all. Now this promise has been broken for most people.[4]

Something is wrong in our lives. Future security is a major concern.

Not everyone wants to stay in a position or with a firm forever; some do. But people do want to know what the future will be. Corporations have erred on the side of misleading employees. If workers know the truth, they can deal with it. The distrust has occurred not just because people are no longer protected in their jobs, but because they are being lied to about possible layoffs and also because when it does happen, there is very little warning or assistance given. Firms have a responsibility to be honest to all workers.

I clearly remember my experience with computers replacing individuals back in 1983 when I was in London visiting the London Stock Exchange. I was invited onto the floor of the Exchange because I actually owned my own brokerage firm. England was not as entrepreneurial as the United States. It was unusual for one individual to own and operate a stock brokerage firm, especially unusual for a woman. There I was on the floor being escorted by and introduced to various brokers and jobbers, London's equivalent of our exchange specialists who are the individuals who actually buy and sell the stocks on the exchange. My entourage grew as I proceeded around the floor. The fact that I was the only woman on the entire floor I'm sure explained some of the attention. But the real thrill came as the crowd subsided and I became engaged in an intense conversation with a small group of brokers and jobbers concerning NASDAQ, the computerized system of the Over the Counter market. London had adopted a system modeled after NASDAQ which forecast the demise of the old way of the face to face dealings of the jobber or specialist system. I was explaining how using the computer and telephone can be a viable way to do business since it is the way I had done business for years, both as a trader for my own firm and as a broker.

The thought of replacing in-person interactions with machines was threatening to these men, just as eliminating the telephone and replacing it with the computer is threatening to many today. It takes a different way of thinking, a commitment to trusting people in order to rely on a machine instead of a person. We have replaced not only face to face communications with voice interactions, but now the computer replaces the personal voice with impersonal computer transactions. Fourteen years later, in 1997, it still takes a different way of thinking in our ever-changing business environment. It takes a commitment to trust the employees and be honest with them about the future of their job.

Unions

Corporations cannot concentrate their energy on the skilled workers. Unskilled and service workers make up an increasingly large percentage of the population. There has been more press recently about the resurgence of unions. Workers are feeling the need to band together for protection. Unions had lost some of their clout. Now, the trend may be reversing. Union membership dropped from 1985 to 1995, despite growth in the labor force. But there is a resurgence of union activity in view of the plight of workers who are struggling economically and who are looking for help. Management must realize that many workers are disgruntled and feeling insecure. It is an increasing problem. The importance of the skilled worker, downsizing, new developments, and the resurgence of unions all combine to force employees and employers alike to assume responsibility for a better future.

AREAS OF CAUTION

There are three areas of caution resulting from the current changes. The split between the rich and the middle and lower wage earners is increasing. People understand this and are beginning to resent it. As pointed out earlier in this Chapter, 98% of the increase in personal income since 1983 has gone to the top 20 percent of the workers. If this inequity continues, there will be unrest and reper-cussions. The majority of the people will not allow a small percent-age of the population to win at their expense. It is not that the rich should not make money; but there is no justification for one group to improve their lives at the expense of all others. That scenario never works, nor should it. The main reason for this phenomenon is the rise of technology. It is not just within this country, of course, that this division is happening. Countries are dividing into haves and have nots and the determining point is access to technology.

Part of the problem within the income gap is the increasing service sector. The top group of high income earners tends to be in the highly trained technology arena. This leaves the service workers earning smaller amounts. We need to acknowledge the importance of the service arena. Not everyone can be a top computer-related worker. The large contingency of workers needed to support our economy must be honored. This refers to service people such as minimum wage earners working at fast food restaurants as well as to teachers, police, and counselors. It is the largest segment of our work force. Even though the computer impacts all of these workers who need training to keep abreast of the changes, these workers rarely reap the monetary rewards of the computer age.

If we believe in abundance and if we trust that the world is improving, we might be able to step back and realize that there is a way to deal with the disparity of wealth. As one example, we need to address the fact that our teachers, especially the ones training our youngest, need some incentives. Business tends to be very critical about the quality of the public school education. As a former high school teacher and administrator in the public schools, I feel much of that criticism is justified. But it is rarely the individual teachers that are at fault. I have been out of the public school system for almost 20 years, but I recently taught a group of public school teach-ers and was reminded about their dedication and commitment to teaching despite great odds. We need to identify those who perform valuable services and figure out how to have those jobs receive pay equivalent to their importance and value. Computer, computer-related companies, and financial industry companies cannot be the only ones benefiting from this new era.

The third warning connected with this new era is that of deifying the computer. The computer is both a solution and a problem. *A National Geographic* article summarizes this view in saying, "One trend is clear: A growing cultlike faith in information, a belief that if we hook up to the Internet we'll be smart."[5]

This same article quotes the statistic that young Americans spend about as much time in front of TV as in school. The average adult watches at least 30 hours of television every week. Our preoccupation with information gathering, even if it is the nightly situation comedy, illustrates that we put a large amount of faith in the validity of that machine and the information we are deriving from it. The computer screen is the next TV, or at least the adjunct to it. Neither of these bode well for relationships unless we understand the new role of interacting with others on computers. The Internet does offer "chat rooms" and email, as well as other interactive opportunities. The outcome of this is unknown. What is known is that if we allow the computers to occupy as much time as we have allowed our television to do with similar results, there is less hope for our future. The answer is not just to view television less or to limit our use of the computer and its Internet access. The answer is to be aware that the machines are tools. They are not our salvation; they do not give us the solutions. But they can provide access to the solutions. It is about using them to our advantage, not allowing them to unproductively dominate our lives. It is a matter of balance.

This transitional age with its advanced technology is providing us the tools to change our economy from one of scarcity to one of abundance, to put people, not machines, back into the center of importance, and to bring power and control back to the individual. If we pay attention to the extreme inequality of wealth, the needs of the service worker, and the dangers of allowing computers to be all consuming, we can shape this transition into a better future.

2

SCIENTIFIC POSSIBILITIES

OVERVIEW OF SCIENCE

If the goal is to trust in a better future, how does science impact that process? Science is, after all, the body of laws and principles that governs our lives. We usually don't think of it as integral to our lives; yet, in fact, our lives are driven and dominated by science.

The agricultural revolution, lasting until the mid 1800s, was replaced by the industrial age after science discovered, among other things, the concept of using energy to create work; that is, replacing the human with a machine. The first law of thermodynamics showed that work can be obtained from heat. The step from this scientific theory to actually constructing an engine capable of converting heat to work was a long, slow process. Yet the construction of the steam engine led to the industrial revolution.

So science brought about industrialism, evolving from pure science to a technology that changed our lives. It is interesting to see this progression on a continuum with science at one end and consumers at the other end. A scientific idea leads to technology, which is simply applied science. This technology is then translated into our everyday businesses, with the computer being the most obvious example. Business then uses the technology to create a new product or service which is sold to the public. This continuum is one way of viewing business in relation to science.[6]

It is important to see the relationship between what we believe today and the scientific theory behind it. Our business concepts are not separate from the rest of the world; there is an interconnectedness that has been forgotten. Not only are ideas and concepts connected; they are also changing. As our knowledge of the physical world changes, our belief structure shifts.

Baby boomers were brought up with science as an integral part of our lives. We were born in the aftermath of the atomic bomb. We were youngsters as Sputnik was launched and then we became part of a school system that stressed science so our country could catch up with the Russians. Science became our god. We demanded proof for everything and if there were no scientific proof, then an idea or concept was not valid.

The push for science in the schools was an end result of the overall emphasis on science in our society, not just in our struggle with Communism. Remember the continuum concept. Ideas begin in science, are applied in technology, are translated to business and they are presented to the consumer or public in some usable form. By the time students felt the effects of science as a reaction to the decline in the race to outer space, much had happened. As Lawrence Krauss, the author of *Fear of Physics,* describes it, "what science does is change the way we think about the world and our place within it."[7] To see this in an historical perspective, it is necessary to look at a brief history of physics, a study of the physical, or natural, and material world. Krauss explains that, "on the surface, the world is a complicated place. Underneath, certain simple rules seem to operate. The goal of physics is to uncover these rules."[8] In looking at our world and how it operates, physics is the science to access.

CLASSIC PHYSICS

Four hundred years ago Galileo created modern science by describing motion. Early technology such as navigational instruments, the mechanical clock, gunpowder, metallurgy and papermaking produced results without a knowledge of the basic laws or principles involved. Kepler, a contemporary of Galileo, tried to understand the world through mathematics. He used the repetition of testing theory against observation to provide a model for modern science.

The most important person, however, in pre-20th century physics was Sir Isaac Newton who, in 1667, showed that the motions of the universe can be described by basic mathematical relationships that were considered to be valid anywhere in the universe. This gave physics a foundation that it never had before. Newton's published work in 1667 is still viewed as the greatest and most influential scientific work ever written, a fascinating statistic in view of all the modern work in physics and other sciences. A work over 230 years old can remain basically valid today.

Newton was the dominant physical scientist from the late seventeenth to the early eighteenth century. The post-Newtonian era, encompassing the late eighteenth and nineteenth century, saw Newton's law of gravity and laws of motion become the basis for the creation of a vast mathematical superstructure. Other branches of physics, such as optics, electricity, magnetism, and thermodynamics grew more slowly and evolved independently of Newtonian mechanics. Although within this span of 150 years there were many significant developments, the fact remains that Newtonian physics was the basis of classic physics by the mid-nineteenth century.

IMPLICATIONS OF CLASSIC PHYSICS

Newton became a symbol of the Age of Reason. As explained by Krauss:

> Newtonian mechanics implied complete determinism. The laws of mechanics imply that one could, in principle, completely predict the future behavior of a system of particles with sufficient knowledge of the positions and motions of all particles at any one time.[9]

Newtonian physics led to the extremes of the industrial era where it was believed that between machines and reason, all life could be explained. Universal laws were accepted. Viewing the world as deterministic and predictable, society began to formulate the view of the perfect world where logic ruled.

Newtonian mechanics was applied to astronomy and eventually led John Couch Adas and Urbain Jean Joseph Leverrier in 1846 to discover the planet Neptune. They did it through mathematical calculations, not through observation. This showed that abstract scientific theory could be used to find planets that were not even suspected. With this discovery, science was hoisted, in people's thinking, to the level of religion. Science could do anything. This event, in some ways, marks the culmination of our extreme belief in science, in rational thought, and in mathematics.[10] The repercussions of this belief are still being felt today.

This theory of 1667 affected all aspects of our lives and is mirrored in everyday life. One such example is the relation to 20th century architecture. *The New York Times* article in 1996 talks of the "conventional view of architecture as the art of putting an orderly public face on things." Even in architecture, "in theory, at least, the modern movement took its cue from industrial technology. The standardized, the rational, the functional: modern architects embraced values they took to be consistent with scientific objectivity."[11]

EINSTEIN AND QUANTUM PHYSICS

Newton, who discovered the theory of gravity and explained the three laws of motion, is rivaled in modern science only by Einstein. By the time Einstein began his work, there were discrepancies being observed in Newton's theories. The first was that Newton had defined an absolute time and space. Einstein showed that neither time nor space are absolute and he combined time and space into a single physical entity called time-space. Newton's laws also stated that any object can travel at any speed so long as the necessary force is used to accelerate that object. But Einstein showed that nothing can travel faster than the speed of light. These discoveries were part of Einstein's theory of special relativity published in 1905.

Einstein went a step further in the unification process and combined the mass, energy, and momentum of a particle into a mass-energy-momentum entity. He applied his general theory of relativity to the entire universe and "opened up vast new domains to the physicist, which encompass not only the structure of the universe but also the structure of most of the elementary particles."[12]

Einstein's work led to quantum physics. Earlier in this chapter, the following quote was used:

> Newtonian mechanics implied complete determinism. The laws of mechanics imply that one could, in principle, completely predict the future behavior of a system of particles with sufficient knowledge of the positions and motions of all particles at any one time.

Quantum mechanics changed this determinism. No longer could one make accurate predictions. The result was that science was based on new rules. "And the rules are that inherent, and calculable, measurement uncertainties exist in nature."

The two great theories of the 20th century, the theory of relativity and the quantum theory, unite our macroscopic world of stars and galaxies with the microscopic world of elementary particles. These two theories "teach us how the expansion of the universe itself can be deduced from the properties of the elementary particles that constitute the matter and energy in the universe."[14]

IMPLICATIONS OF THE NEW PHYSICS

Scientific research begins with theories to prove very specific phenomenon, followed by a drive toward universal principles that leads to a generalization of those laws. By the nineteenth century, this had been taken to the extreme. The new physicists had to acknowledge that they were dealing with symbols, not reality in their scientific quests. In quantum physics, scientists are often dealing with objects that not only can't be seen under microscopes, such as electrons, but with objects that have no mass, such as neutrinos. A particle with no mass is a difficult concept to comprehend.

In the 1950s, after the Atomic Bomb and in the era of Sputnik, we thought science could solve all problems. Again, this was the belief in science as supreme. But gradually, we became as disillusioned with science as with all other parts of our lives. That disappointment is really just a reflection of the extreme that scientists themselves had discovered. Science could not provide a definitive answer. We encounter examples of this attitude in a variety of places. One such example is a comment from a nonscientific source, Sidney Lumet, movie director of *Serpico* and 37 other films:

I remember when science was promising us everything . . . Science, you see, has continually failed us.

We keep winding up with the worse of science. Atomic energy was suppose to liberate us, and now we don't even know where to bury the waste that atomic energy has produced. As we advance medically, we are discovering that some germs have become immune to antibiotics. We have cured old problems only to find that we have created new ones. So I don't quite have the faith that the scientific world will solve human problems.[15]

Mr. Lumet reflects how many of us began to feel. It is part of the general distrust we are experiencing. We no longer trust science. We had expected science to be what it is not; we wanted the discipline to clearly explain our lives. We now understand this field can't do that, partially because of its continual change. We must understand that science reflects the latest theory, not necessarily the final theory. But as we discovered and, as is clearly evidenced in the contrast of the old and new physics, science is a growing, changing study. Scientists are constantly searching for unification in the universe; but in that quest, there are often only partial answers.

Thanks to the media, we are able to keep track of some of the latest discoveries. One such example helps to show the changing face of science. *The New York Times,* in January 1996, reported that quarks, thought to be elements of matter and indivisible since they were named in 1963, may contain even smaller components. The work being done at Fermilab in Illinois was based on a four-year study.[16] If the analysis is accurate, " a whole new level of material existence would stand revealed." Such new scientific information is continually coming to light to change what was once an accepted theory.

Science is, as John Casti in *Complexification: Explaining a Paradoxical World Through the Science of Surprise* says, " more a verb than a noun."[17] It is not static; it is continually changing. We need to remember this aspect and not expect any scientific fact to be a final decree. When we look to science, we must accept change as a reality. New discoveries are explaining why people lost faith in science. Going to extremes is not the answer. Science provides data that can lead to solutions. It does not provide all the answers and it certainly does not always provide definitive explanations. I'm not sure I was ever taught that in school. I assumed what I learned was fact. I never understood that what I learned was only the fact up to that time period.

Only in doing research for this book did it make sense to me that one of the reasons I had lost faith in the world was I had expected my life to be one of order: work hard, get results. When my world fell apart, there was nothing to hold it together. It shattered all of my illusions about what life was suppose to be like. I was a baby boomer, brought up to believe in a logical, rational world. My earlier disillusionment with the Catholic Church left me with no spiritual base and when rational failed, I felt I was left with nothing. The research on physics, however, helped me understand intellectually what had been happening to me. The research also gave me an explanation I hadn't expected. The new theory, chaos, with that unlikely name, lead me to a new intellectual level of comfort.

CHAOS THEORY

It is exciting to be living in a time of transition and experiencing many significant changes firsthand. One such innovation is the chaos theory, which is still being defined. We are watching it being shaped. The chaos theory began in the 1960s with the realization that quite simple mathematical equations could become very complex, and that tiny differences in input could create a very different output. Then in 1975, Mitchell Feigenbaum at the Los Alamos National Laboratory discovered that in a tiny change producing a significantly different result, there was unexpected order. The word "chaos" is misleading since the theory shows that what seems like disorder in a system actually leads to order. The 1970s saw various disciplines, from chemistry to meteorology, studying the theory.

The chaos theory represents the idea that within the defined boundaries of a complex system, there can be random disorder. This chaos is described as:

an intricate mixture of order and disorder, regularity and irregularity: patterns of behavior which are irregular but nonetheless recognizable as broad categories of behavior, or archetypes, within which there is endless individual variety.[18]

Business writer Margaret Wheatley describes that it is natural for a system, whether human or chemical, to attempt to quell a disturbance when it first appears. But if the disturbance survives, then the process begins again, going from stability to instability.[19] This process eventually creates a new order within the system, which will, at some point, also face disturbances. Some of these disturbances will be stopped and some will go on to create further chaos. This theory was the basis of the Nobel Prize in Chemistry won by Ilya Prigogine in 1977, and relates to most disciplines.

There are significant aspects to such a theory. One relates to the terms "linear" and "non-linear" relationships. A linear relationship has one cause and one outcome, is considered a simple relationship and defines a simple system. In a non-linear relationship, one cause may have many different outcomes, or one outcome may have many causes; it is complex.

A second condition of chaos is that a non-linear system is more than the sum of its parts. A complex system can't be studied in parts or in isolation; a scientist can't break a system apart to understand its sections and then put it together again with a knowledge of that system. A non-linear system requires a holistic approach in which the pattern of the behavior of the whole, not the individual parts, is significant.

The new theory is also an interdisciplinary one. One example is the Santa Fe Institute which was established in 1986 to study the links between the simple and the complex in life. "The idea behind the institute," according to President Ed Knapp, "was to break down the barriers between scientific disciplines, to encourage researchers in different fields to work together and to begin to understand what they have in common."[20] Another intriguing aspect of this theory is that it deals with elements on a human scale. The other two post-Newtonian concepts in science dealt with either cosmic proportions as a result of Einstein's theory of relativity or the invisible, hardly comprehensible proportions of quantum physics. Science had seemingly ignored our lives, and anything too common, such as the study of clouds, was too mundane for real scientists. Chaos brought back a human perspective.

Most scientists acknowledge the theory of relativity and quantum physics as the two most significant discoveries of the 20th century. Many are adding chaos, or the more general term, complexity theory, to that elite group.

IMPLICATIONS OF THE CHAOS THEORY

If there is, in fact, order beneath the seeming chaos in systems, can this affect our economic system and our businesses? Conventional economics assumes that in a system of supply and demand, prices will level off at the point at which supply equals demands. "Recently, maverick economists, like Brian Arthur of the Santa Fe Institute, have argued that this is not at all the way the real economy works."[21] Conventional economics was basically influenced by classical physics which assumed there were structurally stable systems. New theories are suggesting that not all systems, such as economics, are stable. They attempt to provide a framework for these new systems that are described as "open" and complex, in comparison to the largely-studied "closed" and simple systems.

I recall when I first entered the financial industry from an educational background and tried to reach an understanding of economic theory. I assumed that if I read enough, I would find the long-term rules that applied to investing. But the more I read, the more I found that there were no rules that worked. There was no way to predict or have a real understanding of what would happen, other than the market would go up and, at some point, come down. Researchers are now proving, as most astute financial analysts already know, that our economic system is complex with no single cause and effect. We have been in a chaotic world, pretending it was structured with understandable rules.

Economics is not the only complex situation with no certain outcome. A British study by David Parker and Ralph Stacey entitled, *Chaos, Management and Economics: The Implications of Non-Linear Thinking* shows that the new theory also impacts how our human organizations function. They use the term "bounded instability" in relation to this theory. Boundaries exist, within which there is order, disorder, then order and disorder in a continual process; this is chaos within a business. Knowing that it is all right to expect the unexpected, and to accept that as natural, can help us see business in a different perspective.

What makes this seemingly chaotic behavior livable is the fact that underneath the random activity is eventually a return to a new order. It is not the same order that was initially in place, but stability in a system does return after a period of disruption. Maybe we can begin to feel more comfortable in our business life, knowing that there is structure underlying whatever modifications we are currently experiencing. We should remember the "bounded instability" and apply it to our lives and our business. Yes, there is instability, but it has boundaries beyond which it will not go. This allows us to trust again. There are limitations and, according to the chaos theory, a new order will arise.

As the new millennium approaches, we are living in turbulent times forcing us to modify the old ways of thinking. An understanding of the role of science adds another dimension. Science discovered the technology that brought us from the agricultural world to the industrial age to the information age. Accepting the scientific basis of this current era furnishes us with a scientific possibility of trust, because the new theory suggests an underlying order to our seemingly chaotic lives.

MY STORY—THE CHAOS THEORY IN MY LIFE

The new brokerage firm I started in 1990, as I stated earlier, failed. I mentioned reasons, but as we learn from the chaos theory, there is rarely one cause to any particular outcome. As a logical person, I always try to analyze situations so that I can understand them in order to learn and not repeat the same mistakes. It was very significant to me when I read and began to understand the scientific aspect, that the complexity of our lives refutes any attempt to simply figure out what one thing went wrong. Think of your own lives and business experiences. In looking back, you will see that rarely was there one cause and effect. There may have been a precipitating event that triggered the final outcome, but in retrospect those events are usually only the last straw, not the total cause. Now I understand that there were many events, some very significant ones, but no one single event that caused the downfall of my firm and my life. A complex situation has complex circumstances.

I was aware after the first month in business that more money would be required. The new focus meant some retraining of these OTC brokers who were used to selling one stock to a client, not emphasizing the total portfolio. Our focus on women meant dealing with people who attended seminars and learned, but often were not ready to make a decision. I found and still do, that women frequently make more sensible investment decisions, but they usually do not make them quickly. Also, the focus on socially responsible stocks attracted too many people not wealthy enough to invest any substantial funds.

The idea of raising additional money to keep the brokerage firm open did not initially pose any problem for me. In the six years of owning and running my first brokerage firm, I had raised money from investors on numerous occasions. This was not new to me. But there were some differences. One was the financial industry environment. As I pointed out, the low-priced stock market had reached its peak in the early 1980s and had begun a slow decline after that. By the early 90s, there was less enthusiasm on the part of investors, those investing in stocks as well as those investing in brokerage firms. In the height of the penny stock market, investors would be anxious to invest in small brokerage firms because they saw the large potential returns. However, a slow market provided lower returns.

The second factor I had not anticipated was the behind-the-scenes workings of some of the people involved in my old firm and within my new firm. Again, a violation of the trust factor. Whether or not there was a stated conspiracy on the part of certain individuals is no longer of any concern to me. What I do know is that private information within my firm was known to outsiders and the information served to sabotage many fundraising efforts. It took me months, however, to understand the impact of those undermining efforts, some of which originated with a key employee within my firm. I know enough of the cast of characters in the events that, even today, if I wanted to know exactly what happened, I could track it down. But what would be the point? Bitterness or anger is wasted energy. Understanding my role in the demise is much more productive and the only thing that serves any useful purpose. What I did learn was that the lack of trust can eventually destroy any business.

My mistakes were, as I have stated, being too optimistic about the future and too trusting. I should have understood that my financial future looked bleaker and bleaker, and was a sign of things to come. Instead, I just plowed ahead doing what I had always done. The saying that if we continue to do the same things we have always done, we will continue to get the same results, applied here. I was hung up on thinking things would always work out because they always had. Yet when there are major disruptions in a pattern, the time has come to reassess. I have learned that when things are too difficult and nothing seems to be happening easily, major changes need to take place. I didn't know that then. I thought that all I could do was run a brokerage firm and I fought to continue to do the only way I knew.

One of my other weaknesses was that I trusted people too much. These events originally caused me to write this book. Trusting people is important, but trusting blindly and expecting them to perform differently than the established norms is wrong. Money, not integrity, motivated too many of the people in the Denver low-priced stock market. I was not discriminating in my support of others. I neglected to observe that not everyone functions on the same ground rules that I did. I learned the invaluable lesson that I was the one who was wrong. I had expected others to think and feel as I do. How many of us have been hurt because of such faulty thinking? I was naive; I didn't look around or listen closely enough to what was really happening. I saw events as I wanted them to be.

Throughout the summer of 1990, I continued my attempts at raising capital for my struggling firm. My brokers were learning new ways of selling and we were trying to raise money for some excellent small companies. But time was running out. Another major event turned the tide.

As many small business owners learn in their process of keeping their doors open, there is an unacknowledged, but accepted way to manage money by writing checks without funds in the bank, knowing that the funds would arrive shortly and cover any checks. I had been doing that type of creative financing for six years. It was not a healthy business procedure, but not an uncommon one for small firms. It is not as easy nor advisable these days since banks have gotten smarter and the consequences more extreme. Unlike now, the penalty for a bounced check was worth the price. I knew how long I had to cover a check because most banks and businesses would send checks through twice and this would allow me at least a week to two weeks before I had to cover the written checks. This is also a banking practice that has changed today. But at the time, it was knowing the business and banking parameters and working within them, even if it meant living on the edge and skirting the rules a little.

In July, I wrote out payroll and rent checks as I had before, without the funds in my business account. At this point, I fully expected one of my two potential investors to provide a check within the next two weeks and I had some backup investors, or so I thought, in case I needed them. Business continued as normal. The one event that I hadn't anticipated, that one event that changed the momentum and began the downhill slide involved the previous owner of the firm I had just purchased. He had received a $25,000 commission check from one of the mutual fund companies. He had to deposit it in the brokerage firm account. He brought in the check and wanted his funds. As banks still do, there would be a hold on such a large out-of state check. At the time, I did not have that much money in my account. I explained that I could not give him a check until his had cleared. I called my bank and asked how long before the funds would be available. They informed me that funds would be released the following Monday. On Monday, the previous owner returned. I gave him a check, and he went to the bank to cash it. Unfortunately, what the bank failed to tell me was that the checks, those I had written prior to my deposit of this large check, had cleared using the funds on hold. If the bank had explained that I couldn't cash the check, but could use it to back checks I had written, I would never had deposited it in that way. So my creative financing scheme, which had served me well for so long, crashed. The money I owed this man was depleted by all the checks I had written. At this point, the money was gone. I couldn't recall the checks. I was as surprised, upset, and shocked as the poor man who expected to cash his check, only to be told that funds were not available.

At the time, even this event didn't overly concern me. After all, I expected investor money momentarily. I had fully expected to cover those checks I had written; now I would just have to cover that one check to this previous owner. I was able to calm him down and assure him my intentions were good. He was a trusting person and had no reason to doubt me. Even though he was angry, he was very understanding and agreed to wait.

Things happened quickly to reestablish the business internally. My remaining employees were totally supportive and we decided to continue and not say die. In hindsight, not one of my better decisions. But I am a fighter, not a quitter. So we struggled on, expecting to either close one of our funding projects or get new investors. All of our remaining creditors were sympathetic and worked with us. We continued on for another 6 months, postponing the inevitable.

3

SOCIAL AND PHILOSOPHICAL ACCEPTANCE

HISTORICAL PERSPECTIVE

Chapter 1 discusses how computers are leading us to an information age in which a new economic view is possible and individuals can become important again. In Chapter 2, we see that physics has discovered a new theory that could provide a sense of order to our chaotic lives. Chapter 3 presents the changes that are occurring in our philosophical and social views. Our thinking is shifting from a "having" to a "helping" mode. This is a continuation of the 1960s concern for others, but is now being espoused by the business leaders, not young rebels.

The current, dominant social view became obvious after World War II brought a time of greater material expectations. The aim of life was happiness and this happiness was expected to lead to harmony and peace. We attempted to satisfy all our wants and desires. Maximum consumption became the creed of twentieth century capitalism. Yet the harmony, external or internal, has never been achieved. The repercussions of this need "to have" are extreme, as described by Erich Fromm in *To Have or To Be?*:

To be an egoist refers not only to my behavior but my character. It means: that I want everything for myself; that possessing, not sharing gives me pleasure; that I must become greedy because if my aim is having, I *am* more the more I *have;* that I must feel antagonistic towards all others: my customers whom I want to deceive, my competitors whom I want to destroy, my workers whom I want to exploit. I can never be satisfied, because there is no end to my wishes; I must be envious of those who have more and afraid of those who have less. But I have to repress all these feelings in order to represent myself (to others as well as to myself) as the smiling, rational, sincere, kind human being everybody pretends to be.[22]

This obsession with " I am more the more I have" led to greed and selfishness. We can question the accuracy of the above statement in relation to our lives and those people we know. Yet the answer is too often affirmative. We tried to justify this behavior by claiming that such action was necessary for the system, and thus good for us. "People refused to recognize that these traits were not natural drives that caused industrial society to exist, but that they were the products of social circumstances."[23]

MONEY

The greed of our society has forced us into an acceptance of success in financial terms of the number and quality of the homes, cars, and toys we accumulate. But as baby boomers who either have plenty of toys or have chosen not to have those toys, we know that there must be more to life. Those things are not enough to make us happy and we recognize that something is missing. "Ours is the greatest social experiment ever to solve the question whether pleasure can be a satisfactory answer to the problem of human existence."[24] We learned firsthand that external pleasure is not a satisfactory answer. This is a positive step; we have experienced what does not work. Now we need to find what does solve the question of human existence. We are beginning to search for a new definition of success and happiness.

Most of us have experienced situations where money dominates. For me, the financial industry showed the lesson well. As new brokers were trained in the penny stock market, they were encouraged to set goals. Those goals were always monetary ones. My ex-partner became a role model for many of the younger brokers because he had a million dollar house, a Mercedes convertible, a beautiful wife with expensive clothes and jewelry, and any other trimmings he desired. This was the model. As brokers began to earn money, they were helped to obtain bank loans for new cars. This meant that they were forced to produce big numbers each month to keep up payments. They had pictures of their next dream car tacked up by the phone. They were on their way. At the time, I didn't real ize how insidious this role modeling and "help" was.

The ramifications of such promotion were devastating for more than one broker who found that money was not her or his only motivation. This also played a role in my losing the firm to my partner. He represented success because he had the money. I had less external success; therefore I was not someone to follow. I certainly acknowledge that being faced with the prospects of making a lot of money, I got caught up in the greed factor. It was easy to set money as the sole motivation and numb myself to other, nonphysical needs. Most of us have had instances in our lives when we decided what price we were willing to pay for some of our actions. At times, many of us chose actions for which we paid an even greater price later— a price that depleted our moral character, not our bank account.

I saw the same obsession with money exhibited in the movie, *Barbarians at the Gate,* based on the book of the same title. This is the story of the RJR Nabisco takeover. What amazed me about this story when I first viewed it in 1992 is how clearly the movie illustrated so much of what I had personally experienced in the stock brokerage business. The extravagance in furnishings, dress, and objects at the Wall Street firms and homes, illustrated in the movie, were just a larger scale of what I had seen in Denver. What really amazed me was that some of the characters were just different versions of ones I had known. A specific example was one of the men who did some work at our firm. His favorite word was "fuck", and it would come out of his mouth at least every third sentence. The word is offensive, especially used to excess. The man was an intelligent person, yet his language certainly did not reinforce that fact. In the movie, one of the key players used the same word and used it almost as often. It was like watching a rerun of my old firm—only the names and faces had been changed. I was amazed at the similarities. Excessive motivation, evident in both my firm and in the movie, can often lead to excessive greed. Then people become pawns to the system. Wall Street firms were dealing with billions and we were dealing with millions. Only the number of zeros was different; everything else was surprisingly similar. Greed has a common denominator.

This concept of money reminds me of the adage "money is only a convenient way to keep score." That line seems to sum up how success is defined in business; money has been the only way to keep score, to tell us how well we were doing. There has been no other socially acceptable way to judge our accomplishments. Most people go after the money, realizing after they have accumulated a great deal, that dollars only represent a way to gauge the extent of one's success. As a society, we have never provided another motive or measurement.

Money is the main criteria we use for our success and our self image. To be all right, to be a good person in our own eyes has become, too often, equated with being financially successful. But the other extreme has also come into play. The idea of money being the assessment of success or self-esteem became an anathema to many. Money then became the scapegoat and poverty was the result. This is not a better scenario. Whether an excessive amount or a lack became the measurement, the result was that money had become the standard. We elevated money to a very powerful symbol.

We need to take money off that pedestal. Money is simply a means to an end, a vehicle to achieve our desires. Money is not a bad thing, but the improper use of this object becomes negative. We need other values, other measures of our self-esteem. Money was the main message of the 1970s and 1980s. The 1990s find us looking for a substitute.

THE CURRENT ENVIRONMENT

Fortunately, there is hope in our search for new answers about our view of society and our definition of success. In the realm of research, the past decades saw biologists and anthropologists regarding humans as basically selfish creatures, motivated by heredity to compete aggressively. But recent studies of higher animals have shown unselfish, cooperative behavior. As was pointed out in a 1996 newspaper article, "Nurturing comes naturally", a zoologist studying chimpanzee behavior claims that the traditional view of people and animals as hopelessly self-centered is wrong. Previous scientific research mainly favored the study of aggression and anti-social behavior. Scientists are now questioning these old ideas and beginning to focus on studies of cooperation. [55]

Other changes in society can be seen in popular literature and new business trends, as reflected in seminars and workshops. One author and speaker who exemplifies this new movement is Stephen R. Covey. Covey points out that in the first 150 years of literature published in the US, the focus was on "Character Ethic" or such principles as integrity, humility, courage and justice. But World War II brought a change and for the last 50 years, "Personality Ethic" with a more superficial success image dominated. He suggests that this focus has led us, perhaps inadvertently, to forget our basic foundation. He points out, similar to Fromm, the futility of trying to live a facade that does not agree with our basic character, our "basic goodness."

Covey brings us back to a positive view of ourselves, one we need to reincorporate into our lives and our businesses. Who we are communicates more than anything we say or do. We trust people when we know their character. He refers to the principles that transcend any religion, social belief, or ethical system. These principles may be temporarily lost because of social conditioning, but they are part of us. These principles, such as integrity, human dignity and fairness, are now making a comeback. Covey shows that it is possible to successfully promote integrity and principles, an indication that the tide has turned. Not only are we ready to return to lost values, but we are openly admitting so and asking for help through literature and seminars.

PHILANTHROPIC AGE

I like the term, "philanthropic age," to describe our new social view in these transitional times. The trend reflects the many business owners, both current and retired, who want to give back to the community in an active, not passive role. Although philanthropy has been around for a long time, donations were mainly in the form of money. The active role, the one I see prevalent today, is contributing time, energy, and expertise, along with money. It is another indication that we are willing to help and trust people again. Within one year, I encountered six specific examples of philanthropists that define active participation. These people show that service to others is being reintroduced in business.

The first example is a man who made his fortune in a nationally known candy company. He helped set up a corporate foundation. What impresses me continually about this man and everyone I have met in connection with this foundation is their real interest in working with the universities and nonprofit organizations that they fund. Among other activities, a main focus is promoting entrepreneurship. They are actively involved in helping students and entrepreneurs be successful with a hands-on approach. They are genuinely nice people whose help is never obtrusive as long as the agreed upon objectives are met. This man is a forceful and delightful speaker concerning the need for entrepreneurship training. His arguments on how the universities are failing to meet this need are powerful. His comments are honest, sincere, and directed at trying to improve the system. He does his philanthropic work because he believes in his cause. His rewards are the satisfaction of helping others and promoting change.

Another example of a business person helping others with time and energy is a manager of a national stock brokerage firm. This manager fits the definition of an all-around nice person. He is not doing good as part of his retirement. He is currently very much in the midst of his career. Yet he made a commitment to help train public school teachers about economics and entrepreneurship after watching his kids learn more about communism in school than about our country's economic system. He has spent considerable time raising money and helping to organize a chapter of the national organization devoted to teaching economics in the schools. Again, this is about active, not passive assistance. He is not just donating money or sitting on a board. He is involved in all aspects of the training and even teaches one of the classes. He is a person who functions with integrity. His brokers know they can trust him. He is not just talking personal responsibility and integrity; he is living it as a successful person doing it at the height of his career. I find him all the more admirable because his success is in the financial industry, one in which greed tends to dominate.

Another example of philanthropic work shows a variation on the theme. The president of a regional supermarket chain helps entrepreneurs get started in his industry. Anyone who has ever tried to sell a new product to a large retail food chain knows how competitive and complicated that process can be. It is extremely difficult for a small producer to break into the system. This president teams up with local nonprofit organizations to train small entrepreneurial ventures who could benefit from access to retail information. I was amazed to learn that most of these products would never make it into the stores without the assistance of this program. In addition, one of the banks provides loans to the participants in the program. The course was created by the president. His corporation pays for the instruction and any other costs, such as weekly dinners for the participants of the class. This is not just a self-serving way to get new products in the stores. The corporation has access to more than enough new products already. There is not even a requirement for a participant to sell in their stores, or to sell exclusively in their stores. It is really about helping the new producer and providing any and all assistance required. The president created a hands-on program. He asks his top managers to spend whatever time is required by the participants. The commitment of the corporation is admirable. He is another example of someone who cares, who goes beyond the normal limits, and who is willing to help others in an area that would not otherwise be accessible. In addition, he has the other quality I used as a criteria for inclusion in my list of philanthropists; he is a kind and trustworthy individual.

The next example of a business person representing the new values we need in our society is a vice president of one of the major automotive firms. In a class that I taught at the University of New Mexico, I was fortunate to have this guest speaker as part of the University's program called, "Experience Teaches" which brings in industry leaders to address the students. At the time, my cynicism had me questioning whether this large corporation executive would have anything significant to say to these students who were expecting to go out and start their own small companies. My judgmental and stereotypical thinking was proven wrong. The vice president gave one of the best and most inspirational class presentations. When he discovered that the class was entrepreneurial, he quickly sifted through his foot-high stack of overheads and rearranged his talk and visuals to fit the audience. Even though I was impressed with that audience-sensitivity, I was even more impressed with one of the main themes of this talk.

To my surprise, he stressed "core values" and discussed many of the changes happening at his corporation in a very favorable light. In addition, he stated that the companies who will create the future are the rebels, the subversive ones, and the ones willing to live on the edge. I find this very refreshing talk coming from a large corporate executive and it gives me hope for his company, who has such executives, and for other large companies. His words and his personality convinced me that the words he spoke were more than just words; he believed them. I walked away with the understanding that even large corporations have executives who understand what needs to be done differently in business today. A top automotive executive was willing and enthusiastically able to talk about basic values to a group of students about to enter the business world. There are changes happening; a different message is becoming evident. Perhaps successful corporations are really starting to understand what needs to happen in this transitional time. In this new era, we must be open to changing our opinions about companies and people as part of the "people-centered" direction of the twenty-first century.

Another example is the man who started a nonprofit organization that trains corporate executives on new management concepts, using the latest in scientific and management research. This is the only organization I know that uses an approach emphasizing the thinking process in business as well as decision implementation. During my first meeting with the driving force behind this idea, I saw that he really cares for people and that he functions on trust in business. In addition, he commits major funding to this project which requires not only money but a significant time commitment for himself, key members of his staff, and other selected, paid professionals. The quality of all the people I met was inspiring. They welcome and understand the need for trust being reintroduced back into business. The group reflects their leader. He is an innovator who is actively encouraging a creative approach to management based on new research, as well as setting a personal example of integrity and ethics in business.

A final example is two of my students at the University of New Mexico. In my entrepreneurial class, students were allowed to work on their own business ideas. In 1996, 15 of the 25 students in my class worked on plans for their own company. This new generation of well-educated entrepreneurs is a very positive sign. In this particular class, these two students did a project on their company that intended to publish moral stories for youth. Listening to two men under age 25 report to the class how their stories, intended for elementary up to high school students, would help promote the values that are missing in our youth today, was refreshing. An isolated incident? I think not. Not only are our current business leaders promoting values and helping others, but also some of our future leaders are already doing the same.

We are beginning to remember our responsibility to help others. This is clearly illustrated in an unusual way in the Disney movie, *The Lion King*. One key scene is when the young lion king Simba, dealing with guilt from the past and trying to avoid making a decision for the future, is told by his father's ghost, "You are more than you think you are" and the even more powerful, "Remember who you are!" We are all more than we think we are. We are not selfish individuals motivated only by pleasure and greed. We are kind, caring individuals who want to help others as part of our successes. We are beginning to rise above the negatives and embrace the idea of service to others. The message in the movie is for all of us, not just for the kids. We are all trying to remember who we are. We are not only remembering, but acting on that remembrance.

The information age provides the possibility of moving from the pleasure-seeking, selfish drive of the industrial era. Studies have shown that cooperation, not competition may be a dominant human trait. Popular literature and speakers are extolling an emphasis on character rather than on an external image. Our success is being challenged by a feeling that "something is missing" in the current financial definition. Individual business executives in large and small corporations are setting new examples of social consciousness with personal involvement. Our movies are prodding us to remember and our literature is showing us how to remain optimistic. Society, reflecting these changing views, is opening the door to trust.

PART II

DEFINING TRUST IN THE WORKPLACE

People often comment that the word "trust" has become meaningless in business. Webster's dictionary defines trust as "a firm belief or confidence in the honesty, integrity, reliability, and justice of another person or thing; faith; reliance." But there is a distinction between trust, belief, and faith, words seemingly interchangeable in the above definition. "Belief" is the broadest application and implies a mental acceptance of something as true. "Faith" implies complete, unquestioning acceptance even in the absence of proof, especially acceptance not supported by reason. "Trust" implies assurance in the reliability of someone or something, often an intuitive assurance. The difference in the three is that belief is a mental acceptance, faith is an unquestioning acceptance, and trust is more of an intuitive acceptance. The three words will be used interchangeably in this text. The emphasis, however, is on "trust" as opposed to faith or belief since the book encourages intuitive and inquisitive, not just intellectual or unsupported, reliance.

Three essential components of trust in a business setting that will be discussed in the next three chapters are trusting oneself, trusting others, and trusting an ethical standard.

4

TRUSTING ONESELF

TRUSTING ONESELF

Trusting oneself seems like the simplest of tasks, yet when examined, is not easy for most of us. Trusting implies accepting and loving the self. We may claim a personal acceptance, but our actions belie our words. Historically, here are some reasons.

Until the 1960s, academic psychology was dominated by behaviorists, such as B.F. Skinner, who believed that only external behavior was objective and could be studied. Emotions and all inner life were not appropriate for science. This reflected the mechanized and standardized era. In the 1960s, the emphasis turned to the study of the mind and the nature of intelligence; but again emotions were ignored.

Fortunately, the pattern of change explored in other aspects of science is also evident in psychology. The last decade has seen unprecedented studies on emotion. New brain-imaging technology has brought to light what happens to our cells when we think, feel, imagine and dream. The irrational is beginning to enter into the lime-light, as in the theory of chaos.

The old emphasis on the rational and mechanical, however, dominates our business actions. In this arena, people are equated with resources. They are often viewed solely for what they can provide for the company, their external worth. This also affects the image of ourselves. If we see others as a resource, how do we see ourselves? The dominant views filter into our psyche and we, too, became commodities that are expendable. We need to deal with ourselves and others as individuals, not as automated cogs. If we follow the newest trends which allow that emotions should and can be studied, then emotions have a place in business. The intellect needs to be balanced with emotions in order to accept the self. Trusting the self implies trusting one's emotions.

TRUSTING EMOTIONS

How do we go about learning to trust our emotions? Self-awareness is one place to start. The past emphasis was on the external, looking and acting better for others. Now there is a shift back to an internal focus, looking within. This means being aware of the self, being aware of moods and being aware of thoughts about those moods. When we are angry in any given incident, we can realize, " I am too angry now to continue talking to this person," and walk away before doing or saying something we might regret. This scenario works both at work and in the home. Accepting oneself is not the extreme of feeling free to express any thought at any time. Accepting oneself implies appropriately controlling those emotions. There seemed to be a period in the 1980s and early 1990s when expressing how one really felt was an important thing to do, without any consideration for the effects on others. Even a boss, who feels justified in yelling at an employee for being in the wrong, is inappropriate if the reprimand is done poorly, in front of others, or in an extreme fashion. The results will rarely be positive. The key to self-awareness is being aware of both thoughts and emotions.

Daniel Goleman, in his book *Emotional Intelligence: Why it can matter more than IQ,* talks of the need to restrain emotional excess. The goal is to balance emotion with intellect, not to suppress either. This brings up one of the recurring themes of this book, balance, which applies to all aspects of our lives and business. A challenge in this new era is to stop the extremes of the industrial era. We have gained nothing if we simply allow the pendulum to swing to the other side and allow emotions to rule. Balance must be maintained.

INTUITION

Intuition is learning to trust those thoughts and feelings that can't always be rationally explained. Even though the intuitive side has historically been attributed to women and never given any real credence, it is more generally accepted today. In the biographies of successful business people, it is surprising how often there are references to following "gut instincts." Intuition is widely accepted as something we all have and use, and needs to be acknowledged in our business dealings.

Intuition is following what we instinctively feel is right, listening to the heart and believing in gut level reactions. Books have been written describing, explaining, and discussing this idea, but a simple explanation suffices. Intuition is trusting our instincts. We all tend to know automatically, in most instances, what we like or dislike. We need to act on those feelings. Machines and computers have forced us into "rational thinking." Intuitive thinking gets us in touch with ourselves. After all the facts and figures are confronted, the final decision in business most often comes on inspiration.

Intuitive thinking means trusting that inspiration. We have abilities and resources within that can absolutely amaze us. We need to acknowledge ideas that just seem to appear, those that seem to float through our minds as we awaken. These are not seemingly crazy flashes; they are often important answers to questions we have been considering. Again, the caution of balance. Today there is much talk of "psychic" abilities. Intuition is nothing abnormal or out of this world. It is simply responding to those thoughts within that "feel right." How often are we sorry that we did not follow what we really "felt" was right and listened instead to what seemed more "rational." Too much external emphasis in business has been placed on the logical, disciplined approach while the intuitive, emotional side, at least outwardly, is ignored.

THE SHADOW SIDE

In order to accept and love ourselves, we need to accept all parts of who we are. Intuition is beginning to get in touch with feelings and the sense of knowing what is right. But there is another part of the picture. There is that other side of us that we wish didn't exist, the shadow side. We have come to think of this shadow side as negative. We tend to live in a world of dichotomies, a world of "either...or." Polarity is a better word to describe how to view the world. Polarity means difference; representing two ends of a spectrum. It is not about determining if people are good or evil, but accepting that we have both of those qualities within us. The shadow part of us can be defined as that which we fail to see or know. We all have hidden thoughts and feelings. The challenge is to understand them and not let them control us.

LOVING OURSELVES

In the 1980s, Robert A. Johnson wrote *WE: Understanding the Psychology of Romantic Love*. In concluding his book, he makes the statement that:

And we can discover, to our surprise, that what we have needed more than anything was not so much to be loved, as to love.[26]

Our greatest challenge is to love, even more than to be loved. This is evident in the increased divorce rates. Couples wed in 1970 had a fifty percent chance of separating or divorcing and that figure increased to 64 percent for couples wed in the 1990s. These statistics do not show a people successful at loving.

Theoretically, there are basically only two emotions: love and fear. Joy, anger, and other emotions are simply variations of either love or fear. This makes life simpler. Fear dominates in our society. We need to look at love. If we love, we are not in fear and vice versa. If we love ourselves, then we are not reacting to situations out of fear which leads us to be defensive and closed.

The affirmation of one's own life, happiness, growth, freedom, is rooted in one's capacity to love; i.e. in care, respect, responsibility, and knowledge. If an individual is able to love productively, he loves himself too; if he can love *only* others, he cannot love at all.[27]

The use of the masculine in this quotation by Erich Fromm dates it to a period prior to the 1990s. Yet the sentiment it expresses is not dated at all. If we can learn to care for ourselves, respect ourselves, assume responsibility for our actions, and understand who we are, we are on our way to loving ourselves.

MY STORY— TRUSTING MYSELF

My life is an example of someone being forced to accept and trust all aspects of the self, even the shadowy ones. Six months after the overdrawn check incident at my new firm, there was still no real improvement in the financial situation. There were many projects that could have provided the necessary funds. But nothing came together. No matter how hard we worked within the firm, only small things fell in place. We had enough money to survive, but not enough to take care of additional problems, such as the $25,000. Then the inevitable happened. The man to whom I owed the money became frustrated, impatient and had me arrested. I was allowed to go to the jail myself and not be taken from my office or home in handcuffs. In looking back on those times, I would never have made it through that situation without the help of Peter, the man I was living with at the time. Peter was both an emotional support and, as times got worse, a financial one. Despite the fact that we are no longer together, Peter and I are still great friends and I cherish that friendship because of who he is and how much he helped me.

Peter went with me to the jail that day. But no one was allowed to accompany me down into the processing room where fingerprints and pictures were taken. I spent considerable time talking to an older couple being arrested on a business-related crime. Their story was more extreme, more unfair, and had more serious consequences than mine. I was reminded that no matter how bad our situation seems, someone else's may be worse. I was surprised to find myself consoling these people and encouraging them as I sat in the police station waiting to be catalogued as a suspected criminal. That helped put the day in perspective for me. After the processing, I had to arrange for bail, which was waived. Then I was allowed to leave and await my court appearance. I hired an attorney who was wonderfully supportive and began the process that would take two years to be resolved. I was being my usual optimistic self and trusted that some early arrangement would be made. After all, even though I was guilty of owing the money, there was no criminal act involved.

At this point it is necessary to digress and look at how this related directly to self esteem. I have had a few years now to think about what had gone wrong, other than the financial problems. The one real clear element is the lack of self-confidence, which had rarely been a problem for me. I had always decided what I wanted, went after it and got it. That had been the story of my life. After two divorces, the break with my business partner, and the financial problems, I had expected that I could overcome anything. But the arrest seemed to be the final straw, the one event I couldn't process into my acceptance of me. On the surface, I was going to fight, win, and go on. But underneath, an insidious self-doubt and self-deprecation had taken hold.

In talking with the attorney, I felt ashamed. Even though my story was clear, there were some hazy business practices. I was told that a jury wouldn't relate to the financial industry or its practices and would view this as a white collar crime that shouldn't be allowed. I understood what the perception problem would be. But I also had a strong belief in the truth.

I wanted to have a trial with the judge only and be willing to let him hear the truth and decide. By the time I suggested this alternative to my attorney, I had been in the courtroom a few times as we were trying to work out arrangements with the district attorney. I had observed the judge and determined him to be fair and open-minded. I watched how he handled the people and saw how he really tried to be understanding and fair. I had respect for him. My attorney, however, convinced me that a trial would be too costly and too risky. Plea bargaining would be best and even though it would mean I would have some record, at least I wouldn't be faced with the prospect of losing the case and potential jail time. If I had not felt beaten, I would have followed my own instincts.

The court process dragged on. During that time, I downsized my firm, moved to smaller offices, and then to my home. I tried everything I knew. I worked on many projects that were excellent and should have worked. I didn't realize at the time what a toll all of the court proceeding were taking on me. I just kept struggling, unaware how far my self worth was falling with each passing day. In the process, we moved back to Santa Fe. I decided to get a job. For me, that was a major step. I had run my own business for over 10 years, working for someone else was hard to imagine. With a doctorate in education and years of teaching, and with my extensive background in all areas of the financial industry dealing with small companies, I should have been able to find a job. The missing factor was my self-defeating attitude. It was not even obvious to me at the time. I am a fighter and a survivor. But the real fight was my own inner struggle with self worth. And I was losing that battle.

SOCIETY'S SHADOW SIDE

Why is it that crime has become the number one issue in the nation? Part of the answer is that historically, times of transition tend to be violent. In order to function in our transitional era, we need to better understand the violence. In order to function better as human beings, we need to understand that aspect within ourselves. I wish the discussion of crime and violence did not belong in this book. But as I learned, crime is an element of our society that cannot be ignored. As a society, we hire more police, build more prisons, and assume the problem will be resolved. Statistics prove otherwise.

Since my court encounter, I have volunteered and worked at a prison with inmates' families and taught entrepreneurship to inmates. This was an eye-opening experience. People are always curious about my work in the prisons. They want to hear about it, attracted and repulsed at the same time by the criminal element. What I learned being in and around the State Penitentiary in Santa Fe, New Mexico was that there really is no division of "us" and "them." I got to know many prisoners and spend enough time with them to learn that despite their crimes, they were people like us. There is a very extreme element of the hardened criminal, the vicious ones who will never be able to function in society, nor should be allowed back in. But these are not the majority. We create prisons to deal with crime. Then we do nothing to help inmates deal with why they were incarcerated in the first place.

Our country has a major problem with our penal system. As

in other instances, we think we can lock up the problem and it will go away. However, the price of thinking that prisons are about security, not rehabilitation, is a prison population increasing significantly each year.

As a humanitarian, I realize we need to address the ever-increasing crime problem and the ever-increasing number of people we put in prison, let out, and put back in again. As a business person, I see clearly that our country will have a problem financing our prison system if the growth continues at its current rate of a 7% increase each year. We literally can no longer "afford", either from a humanitarian or business viewpoint, the current prison trend. If we don't address the recidivism rate, then we are just burying our heads in the sand. The reality is that there is a problem.

In my 18 months working with the prison system, I understood what one of the prison teachers had told me at the beginning. He said that you could tell after a brief period of time which inmates could be trusted and would make it on the outside. I found that to be true. The crime itself was rarely the indicator. In the minimum security facilities, dealing with burglars and small-time drug dealers among an assortment of other criminals, one could fairly easily predict which criminals would keep returning. The statistics show that over 70% of inmates return to jail after their release. In some places, that rate is even higher. So we have inmates who continually return to prison. We pay the price but do nothing to improve the situation, except lock them up each time.

I am not suggesting that any crime should be tolerated or excused. My biggest lesson in this area was taught to me by an inmate who was a murderer. In discussions with him, I learned a very valuable lesson. He would allow no excuse, no sociological escape for his actions. He had killed someone. He would never be able to change that. But he was working on himself. At age 30, after over 10 years in prison, he was about to be released. He was determined to make it when he got out despite the odds against him. His acceptance of his crime and his willingness, not bitterness, to pay the price even though he could never bring that life back, showed me he had a chance. I kept in touch with him after his release. A year and a half later, he was doing very well in society. He is unusual. He fought hard to make it. He succeeded, not because anyone helped him, but because he helped himself.

There were many men and women that I worked with in the prisons who had much lesser crimes and shorter sentences. But I knew they would have a very hard time on the outside because they never accepted that they had done anything wrong. They were just mad that they got caught when so many others didn't. Lack of accepting one's faults, even on this larger scale, is our lesson. This is what makes us like these criminals. The challenge is to acknowledge that sometimes good people do bad things. We have to pay the price for our transgressions, whether it be the small price of a fine, a reprimand or a night in jail, or a large price of years in prison. That is the free choice we have in this country. We must accept that we all make mistakes, many minor ones and some major. We must be responsible for these actions. We think that if we lock away the "bad guys," our own "bad side" won't appear. The bad side, except in extreme cases for which we definitely need prisons, is a natural part of us. If we allow ourselves to feel our emotions, we may not need to act out so many of the crimes. John Bradshaw, the popular TV and author-psychologist talks of how one member of a family "acts" out any of the family secrets. That is exactly what criminals are doing on a large scale. They are acting out our society secrets—those parts of us we want to deny.

When I started working at the prison, I thought I could really make a difference working with the inmates' children and wives, and teaching some of the fathers within the prison. I learned a valuable lesson. The problems go too deep. There is no easy fix. What do you say to young kids who basically expect to go to prison because most of their relatives are already there? What role models do we hold up to them? An athlete who earns $25 million dollars a year? That is not reality for them. Many of our government officials, our corporate executives, and our religious leaders are seen as less than honest and many of them provide no positive role model. The answer is to change the economic system in order to accommodate our values and principles. We have learned since the 1960s that the only way to change anything is through economic strength. Today as business leaders, we have that strength. Our responsibility is to shape the changes that are happening around us. We must become role models for our children, for our society.

The most important message about helping make positive changes in our business world is that we must begin with ourselves. We can't preach one thing and do another. The actual preachers, such as Jim Baker, found that didn't work. We tend to have strong detectors today for the truth. Too often we do not hear honesty. I like the example of the parent who is in the grocery store with her child. The clerk mistakenly gives the parent too much change, an incident obvious to the child. How many of us would walk away, feeling the money was owed to us since the clerk made the mistake? What is the message that is given to our children? When is it all right to take money that does not belong to us? If we don't start with the little incidents in life, we have no right to be self-righteously indignant when we are on the losing end. There is a reason crime and violence are on the incline. It is a complicated issue. It is part of our transitional time. It is evidence of our extremes.

We need to accept responsibility for all of our actions, even the negative ones. If we don't have to lock away our fears, maybe we can begin to trust ourselves again. Dealing with our emotions and balancing them with our rational thoughts could help us on a daily basis. This will impact our lives and our businesses and, over time, the whole of society.

5

TRUSTING OTHERS

TRUSTING OTHERS

Learning to accept ourselves is not easy. Learning to trust others is even more difficult. The industrial revolution created a homogenized society. The corporate structure, reflecting society, has not allowed for differences. Individual strengths are given lip-service, until that individuality conflicts with the corporate code. Rather than berate the corporations as the villains, we need to step back and view the predicament in the context of our societal growth. During the industrial era, we worked hard as a society to accept others and assimilate them into our culture. But in this process, equality became uniformity, sameness became the norm.

Benjamin DeMott wrote a powerful article on race relations in 1996 entitled, "Sure, We're All Just One Big Happy Family." He asks the question, "Why is white America so dim about racial divisions?" and answers that we have accepted the notion that the races have achieved equality because "media images of racial sameness are masking the differences and conflicts."[28] Mr. DeMott is very critical and pointed in this comments. He dismisses the concept of sameness and claims it is time for Americans to wake up from their obliviousness and realize how negligent our lack of awareness has been.

His comments relate to the discussion of our shadow side. We want to pretend everything is fine and we cover up much in order to maintain that deception. It is not just about race, although that issue certainly is a powerful one. The real issue is much larger, encompassing most of our relations with others. There is always a group, whether based on race, culture, gender, or criminal activity, that we designate our scapegoats. Then we feel better about ourselves because there are people worse than we are. But it is time to recognize the extremes of these old views that have insidiously invaded our consciousness. We believe we are right in insisting everyone think, act, and feel as we do. When they don't, we look down upon them. This is the society we inadvertently created as a result of thinking we could standardize our lives. We can't. We are individuals and these differences must be acknowledged.

DIVERSITY

The new word is "diversity." A different effort needs to be made toward accepting others as they are. Trusting others is a crucial part in business. If we accept that it is all right for others to be different, we can trust them. Minimizing differences and allowing them to surface has not materialized strongly in business. The corporate thought is still in the old mode of wanting everyone to be as similar as possible because that makes an organization easier to run. This conformity does not work, as is evident in our business and in society. It is time to openly look at our own prejudices and acknowledge we are either afraid of, or distrust, certain ideas and individuals.

One example of diversity is the male/females differences that have been receiving renewed attention in the press and literature recently. Gender differences are being viewed as simply that, differences. The glass ceiling holding many women back in large corporations is partially the result of women deciding not to become the same as the men in executive positions. Women are realizing that our style of communication is often at odds with the typical male-dominated corporate style. There are some strengths in the way women tend to communicate, and there are some weaknesses. Women often do better with the consensus type of leadership when an agreement can be reached among participants. This style of managing is effective in a team building situation, but in a time of implementing crucial decisions, a hierarchical structure may function better. These generalizations do not fit all instances, which is exactly the point. We need to understand others based on who they are, not based on who we want them to be.

Another aspect to diversity was pointed out in a *Providence Journal-Bulletin* article entitled, "Media, Academia Undervalue Diverse Viewpoints." This article comments that while diversity of race, culture, or gender is being sought in academic and media environments, there is very little effort to get any "diversity of viewpoints."[29] According to the article, we don't encourage diversity in two of our most mind-molding institutions, the university and the media. The standardization model has permeated the way we are taught to think. Cable TV and the Internet are having an impact on this lack of diversity. Technology, which led the way to this "sameness," is leading the way out. We need to infiltrate our institutions that are most immune to new ideas. Economics is forcing changes in corporations but it may take longer to affect these institutions. Yet both the universities and the media, which impact our thinking, must change.

COMMUNICATION

We all have seemingly valid reasons to distrust certain, if not most, other individuals. No discussion is going to convince someone to all of a sudden start trusting another. There needs to be some way for us to begin this process. Trusting others, as in trusting oneself, must start with acceptance. Accepting others can only happen if we understand them. How do we deal with this diversity in order to accept them?

The key word in this process is communication. We really do not communicate well in our society as is evidenced by the number of divorces, lawsuits, and general disagreements in our lives and in business on any given day. Communication needs to be redefined. Too often we think we are communicating when we are talking to another individual. But talking is only one part of communication. Communication consists of talking, writing, reading, and listening. Listening is the aspect that seems the weakest in our society. We believe if there is an argument, all we have to do is explain our position often enough and loud enough and the other person will be convinced. Somewhere along the way to the 21st century, we forgot that other people actually had different and valid opinions. This is the legacy of the age of conformity. In accepting diversity in our new information age, we must accept diversity of opinion. Hopefully, we will not go to the other end of the spectrum and honor every opinion, whether it be justifiable, valid, harmful or not. But we do need to understand others' viewpoints.

Listening is not an easy task. We tend to feel very strongly about our positions. Learning to put our own ideas aside and listen objectively to someone else is difficult. But difficult or not, this simple concept must be implemented. There must be a vested interest on the part of both people to really want to understand the other and to allow both to win. The old concept of win/win is a powerful one. Understanding cannot happen, thus communication cannot take place until both parties are committed to listening. If the only real interest in the interaction is to get the other person to see your side, then one person wins and the other loses.

The concept of win/lose as opposed to win/win is too often prevalent in business. We assume winning is the only way to function. Wars are probably society's extreme example of this concept. We fight for what we believe in. We translate this into business and use war terminology such as "guerrilla tactics," "killer instincts," "the corporate battlefield," and so on. If we continue to promote war-related words, we will continue to see business as a "fight." In such a mentality, there is little room, even in a minor disagreement of the day, for others to win. If someone else wins, then we perceive the situation as if we have lost; losing is viewed as unacceptable. A change from the mentality of win/lose to one in which we accept that everyone can win is necessary in understanding and accepting others. This is related to abundance. If we believe there is enough for all, then "winning" becomes less significant.

Stephen Covey in *First Things First* explains a simple, effective three-step communication process. First, one seeks mutual benefits for all involved. Second, one seeks to understand the other person before trying to get them to understand you. This is the key to the process and perhaps the most difficult since we have so little training for it. In this process of seeking to understand, it becomes less important *who* is right and more important *what* is right. But we must value the other person in order to do this. Listening is the first step. Until we change our attitude about having to be right, there is no real listening going on. Once we open to the other person's viewpoint, we can attempt to explain our position. There is room for synergy to take place. Two people can create a third alternative representing a shared vision, not just the viewpoint of one participant.

This shared vision can be incorporated into business with a little dedication and practice. Too often arguments occur within an organization where the goals should be the same. This three step approach can also be applied to relations with customers and other businesses where the perception of everyone winning is even more difficult.

A crucial element in this process is the attitude connected to it. If everyone understands before being understood, finding an alternative solution is easy. People often refuse to see the value in this process. Unless one is willing to understand, value, and accept others, nothing will work. A willingness to try is all that is needed.

How often in meetings is the viewpoint of the other really considered? Many of us do not listen, but begin formulating our rebuttal as soon as the other person starts talking. Too little time is spent comprehending what any one individual is trying to say. Meetings tend to be long and unproductive with participants giving up trying to express their opinion. Listening is necessary in establishing an atmosphere of trust.

These concepts are not new. In 1936, Dale Carnegie wrote *How To Win Friends & Influence People* which discusses the same basic ideas. There are rarely new ideas, just a repackaging of older ones. Carnegie's book has been a must-read for successful business people for a long time. The message is even more appropriate now. We know what to do; we just aren't doing it.

MY STORY—A NIGHT IN JAIL

There are many reasons why we have learned not to trust others, making the trust factor hard to achieve. My court experience and final sentencing qualify in that category. Catastrophic experiences force us to retreat and then to reevaluate. My experiences reminded me of the difference between trusting everyone and trusting discriminately.

April 1993 was the date of my final court appearance. A plea bargaining had been worked out with the final details to be decided in court. My attorney suggested that I cry to show how really sorry I was. My reaction to this suggestion could cover an entire book about how women are "supposed" to act. I had already experienced a scene in court the previous year where my cool exterior, which worked well in business, was hurting me in court. Men and women are not treated the same in court. As I learned later when I did some volunteer work at the women's prison in New Mexico, women are not expected to do wrong, and are judged and sentenced more harshly when they do. Despite the philosophical debate, I was too sick and emotionally upset that day to try to pretend anything. I didn't have to try to cry in court; I couldn't stop myself. I had plea bargained to a third degree felony for which there could have been a sentence of 4-6 years in jail, but it was waived. The 200 hours of community service was the easiest part of the sentence. I had already been doing volunteer work at the women's prison in New Mexico and I intended to continue. The repayment of the money on a monthly basis was what I had been offering to do since the beginning. What was too overwhelming was the fact that, despite everything, despite the fact that I had not committed a crime, I was being convicted of a felony. This wasn't a misdemeanor, the lesser charge. This was a felony. A convicted felon. I couldn't come to grips with that reality. But reality it was and when the judge pronounced the final part of the sentence, that I was to spend the night in jail—I died inside.

A night in jail. That is what the judge said. If anyone thinks this was an adventure, fun, exciting, or any other positive description, think again. Even when the judge said it would only be one night, my heart sank. I was stunned. I realized that the outcome of my sentencing could have been much worse. But with the circumstances of the case, I didn't expect anything other than probation. My attorney and Peter kept assuring me how lucky I was, but I was not to be consoled. I was physically ill and had been for 3 days. I was exhausted from the emotional strain. I just wanted it to be over.

The only saving grace was that, in the sentencing, the judge said, "This was not a criminal case; it was a civil case." That one sentence confirmed what I knew, but at that point I needed validation. If I had listened to my own instincts, I would have gone before the judge with the case and I would probably have won.

I felt betrayed. I felt sick. I felt alone and I felt awful. A guard motioned me through a locked door to the elevator leading into a tunnel connecting the court to the jail. I realized that I was functioning as if this were a dream. The guard made me turn around to be handcuffed. I was numb. I'm sure I looked normal and maybe even sounded normal as I joked with the guard about the metal gate separating us in the elevator. But I was not normal. I experienced something I had never felt before. I felt disjointed, a sense of being outside of myself. I was two people. The outward me looked and talked fine, but the real me wasn't really there. I was somewhere else since it was too awful to be where my body was.

The situation progressed with the same sense of illusion. I was too sick and too tired to be sensible. I sat in a cell waiting to be processed for six hours. Thank goodness for the other woman in the cell who was also waiting. If I had been alone, I might not have been able to handle the situation. I felt as if I were really close to the edge. I think I understand what it is to be on the brink of insanity—that place where we can't cope with reality so we escape into some other place in our minds. Fortunately, I was not alone.

I was processed, which meant completing the paperwork in order to go into the jail itself. More fingerprints and pictures were taken. Then we had to walk down to get our jail clothes. The idea of giving up my clothes and putting on the jail outfit was pretty upsetting. For the first time in my life I felt violated as the male guard asked me if I wanted a bra or T shirt and what size panties I wore. It was not at all the horror stories I have seen on TV, but at that particular moment, it was as awful. I'll never forget that feeling. I realized I had no say or recourse in the matter. That was the scary part.

Once dressed in my blue top and pants, white T shirt, white socks and slip-on rubber shoes, I was told to wait in another cell before going to the jail. I might have started to calm down, but the guard looked at my sheet and saw that I was in for one day. He told me that one day meant 24 hours from the time I entered the jail, meaning I would be in jail all the next day and into the next evening. I panicked inside. What could I do if they tried to keep me, if I had to stay, if the judge had misspoken when he said I would be let out the next morning—what could I do? Any strength I had left drained away. The guard said he would check this out for me, but never did. I asked a second guard about the time frame. He reinforced what the first guard said. Later, before we were sent to our assigned rooms, I was informed that I would be released early the next morning. I was relieved but still apprehensive. We carried our blankets, towels, toothbrushes and toilet paper in a bed roll. My cell was on the second floor. I had to go back downstairs to get a mattress and pillow.

I remember little of the other women except my roommate. She had been sentenced to a year for drunken driving. Even though this was not her first offense, the sentence was extreme. She had agreed to a plea bargaining, then went to court only to find that the district attorney had changed his mind and she was sentenced to a year. She didn't even have time to go home to get her affairs in order. She had a drinking problem, but had received no counseling and had been depressed for three months. She wasn't bitter; she accepted her responsibility, but was angry at the lack of help. We talked quite a while. It helped her. It helped me. In playing listener and counselor, I could stay out of my own pain.

In the small cell that I shared with her, I was on the top bunk which was almost too high for me to reach. A vent was blowing on me but I was too sick and miserable to move the pillow to the other end of the bunk. The noise kept me awake, but I couldn't sleep anyway.

Lights went on at 6 a.m. I had to wait until they called me. I wanted to be ready, so I sat on the edge of the bunk for the longest time, too paralyzed to move. Finally I jumped down.

I took my mattress and spread it out on the floor, laid down and cried. I had this unfounded fear that I wouldn't get out. When would they call? My cellmate told me that this was her birthday. That only made me feel worse. How could one endure a birthday in a place like this? She had 9 months to go on her sentence, the thought was too overwhelming.

At 8:00 am, they finally called my name. I was taken back to the processing place and after changing back to my own clothes, I walked out, got in the car, and drove home.

TRUSTING THE ORGANIZATION

My experience made me question institutions and organizations. How can we trust systems that simply aren't working for the benefit of individuals? We all have examples of our own personal horror stories whether it be with phone companies, credit card companies, insurance companies, or some other bureaucracy. Each encounter makes us more suspicious; mine did. But it is necessary to step back and look at the bigger picture before entrenching our position.

An organization is an entity with characteristics of its own. Reflecting the chaos theory, organizations are now seen as dynamic systems that will naturally have disturbances which create tension and conflict. This conflict is not only tolerated, but seen as a sign of growth. This new theory is not widely accepted within corporations. Yet this is exactly how businesses have functioned over the years.

Science has shown us that an organization is not simply the sum of its parts. It cannot be separated and its parts studied. There is an interrelation that must be acknowledged. Any business must recognize that shifts will occur with the addition of new personnel and management. The organizational culture must be defined and redefined as changes occur.

Another aspect of an organization is that it must not be viewed as a family. In the past decades, some authors have attempted to suggest that we view the corporation as a unit, interacting much as a family does. But families and businesses have different goals, one is supportive and the other financial. Certain roles overlap, but supervisors should not be viewed as parental figures. Competition should not be seen in the same light as sibling rivalry. Many communication problems arise when people play out familial roles in the organizational setting. Often this is done unconsciously, but the effects are destructive. Much literature has talked about the psychological concept of transference whereby an employee reacts to any criticism from a manager as if a child. Transference is not just a problem for employees. Often it is triggered by managers giving orders and expecting workers to react as they would expect their children to react, especially with the thought of "you don't need an explanation of why, just do what I tell you to do."

These old patterns don't work well in a business setting, but employees are more apt to be tolerant when the corporation treats them with the same security a family provides. Since corporations are no longer providing a future security, employees are no longer willing to allow that tolerance. Now employees expect answers, making everyone more accountable and putting business back into the role of being a business. When a business drops its facade of being a family, it is easier for employees and managers to stop familial reactions to business situations.

What has impacted the integrity of our organizations? The most significant aspect is the lack of personal responsibility. The corporate atmosphere has so permeated the environment that people often function in business as robots, without seemingly being aware of the effect their decisions create. If defective products or dishonest services are not the concern of the corporation, then they are not the responsibility of the individual worker. The 1980s became the extreme of the individual giving up control to the corporation. Employees were involved in products and services that they all knew were inferior. But everyone realized the corporate policy was to pass the inspections and pretend everything was normal and the right way to do business. No one seemed to care that these decisions could adversely affect others' lives.

In writing this book, I spoke to a friend that I had met when I was doing volunteer work at the women's prison in Grants, New Mexico. Alyce relayed how difficult it was to trust anyone in prison. Three years after her release, her feelings are still strong about the fact that no matter how difficult it is to trust other inmates, it is even more difficult to trust the guards. Sexual favors can easily be traded for a drug-free urine test or items from the outside, including drugs. Alyce later discovered that she could not trust the case workers and others assigned to help with her release. These people provided inaccurate information and, in many instances, lied about the procedures.

All of our institutions and businesses have similar problems. Being in prison and unable to trust anyone in authority is an extreme example of how people today are feeling in many corporations. The prisons are a microcosm of much that goes on in society. We must begin to look at the internal abuses that exist. Everyone is aware of them. But as in prison where no one wants to talk about guards who are instrumental in allowing drugs, corporations too often pretend that such things as mistreatment and corruption aren't occurring.

A powerful example of never questioning the system occurred in the Challenger explosion. Even though NASA, a government agency, was in charge, there were many corporations who participated. Two recent books discussing the incident were reviewed in a 1996 *The New York Times Book Review*. One of the corporations recommended against the launch. But NASA had experienced too many delays and didn't want the bad publicity of another one. Both of the books reported that the space agency pressured the managers to change their decision and they did. One of the books, *The Challenger Launch Decision* by Diane Vaughan, explains that when NASA pressured the reversal of the decision, the agency was following previous patterns. The field joint problem had been present on other flights. But NASA launched Challenger because it had been successful launching other dangerous shuttle missions, leaving a false sense of beating the odds again. What I find most interesting is the reason given for this fateful decision. Individual responsibility was nonexistent; the system created the problem. "Individuals erred, not in failing to question the safety of the field joints, but in failing to question the infallibility of the system."[30] The conclusion was that the men who chose to launch the Challenger did so as a result of pressure from the system.

This is an extreme example, but most large corporations could cite similar situations, especially in the 1980s, hopefully with much less drastic results. Does the fact that such incidents were almost commonplace in business excuse the individuals from culpability? That could be a very complicated legal issue.

Morally, the question is less complicated. Rather than try to assess the fault of the past, it is more productive to try to avoid reoccurrence. The 1990s have brought an awareness to the public. Corporations realize they can no longer get away with such activities. We now need to look at what will internally change the system. Corporate executives must give clear messages that incidents, such as the NASA disaster, will not be allowed under any circumstances. But just as important, the individual employee must assume some responsibility. The danger in a corporate culture is that individuals feel so helpless, they give up any control or responsibility. This must change, and can't just be done from the top down, although that is certainly a necessity. Irresponsible actions cannot take place if the individual worker, a thinking, feeling individual who is not a robot, refuses to allow them. Certainly there are consequences for an individual to make a stand against an unfair or potentially dangerous practice within a firm. When are we going to understand that there are also serious repercussions, perhaps physical harm, for the consumer using that product or service? We can no longer say, "That is not my problem." There is an individual concern which then gets translated to a corporate concern. This is not simplistic, wishful-thinking, but is the only way our society will be able to move into the next century with any sense of integrity intact. Each and every one of us must be willing to assume our share of the blame and be an active, not passive, part of the solution. Employees know exactly what activities, practices or procedures need to be changed in order to make an organization trustworthy. There is no longer any reason for not making those changes. Excuses are not justified. If we act now, we can salvage the distinction between right and wrong within the corporations and within our lives.

Fortunately, there are always examples to show that people are doing it right; that they are showing trust, not just mouthing the words. A letter printed in 1995 in *The Albuquerque Journal* from the governors of the New Mexican Indian tribes to Governor Gary Johnson of New Mexico addressed the issue of gambling. The intent of the letter is not the concern here, nor is this intended as either a political or a gambling statement. I use the letter to emphasize the significance of keeping one's word. The letter states, " you have shown you are a man of your word . . . By this letter we express our gratitude, not so much for keeping your word, for in a simpler world a man keeping his word would not be exceptional, it would be expected." It concludes with the following words, "Do not lose your honesty in a time of dishonesty. Do not fall victim to cynical and opportunistic politics. Remain resolute in your belief that great nations, like great men, should keep their word."[31]

Unfortunately, honesty is unusual in politics and in business. But, as pointed out by the Native Americans, we should "not fall victim to cynical and opportunistic" business practices. Before we can trust corporations again, we need to recreate a simpler world where great corporations, and great people, keep their word.

6

TRUSTING IN AN ETHICAL STANDARD

AN ETHICAL STANDARD

It is not enough to understand and trust ourselves, or to accept and trust others. The third aspect of integrity in business is the need for an external measurement. There must be an ethical standard; an objective measure of what we are trusting. There is widespread agreement that such a standard is necessary, but much less agreement on the content of that standard.

There are various theories of ethics. But none of them provide a definitive direction. They are all possible ways to approach ethics. As business people, we need more than theories. We need a practical solution, one that sets the same rules for everyone. This is the biggest problem in the area of ethics—the rules according to whom?

Most colleges teach entire courses on ethics and many corporations are hiring high level executives to oversee ethics. Some elementary schools, in states such as New Mexico, teach "Character Counts" which consists of respect, responsibility, fairness, caring, trustworthiness, and citizenship. There is an emphasis on trust and integrity in businesses, in business schools, and in public schools. But the question remains, what does an executive do to simplify managing ethics within an organization? Is there a clear, workable understanding of ethics?

In Robert Pirsig's novel, *Zen and the Art of Motorcycle Maintenance,* the narrator's quest to define "quality" resulted in his understanding, at the conclusion of the book, that we already know what quality is. He points out that the intellectual exercise to precisely elucidate the term is meaningless. I find this same process applies to ethics. In relation to business, we "know" what is ethical and what is not. We can debate the nuances and attempt to specifically define the boundaries. But there is an inner wisdom that transcends all such exercises and renders them pointless.

We do know what is right and wrong. We know that we should not lie, steal or cheat. The various shades of each of these can become complex, but only if we allow that to happen. We need to remember that being dishonest is wrong, whether we are dealing with customers, employees, or employers. This makes the situation, whatever the dilemma, easy to handle. Everyone within an organization needs to agree on the standards and have the confidence that these standards are being followed and enforced.

A newspaper editorial, written by syndicated columnist Richard Reeves in 1996, entitled "Jaded America Indifferent to Truth" tells the story of a 12 year old private school honor student and athlete who wrote to a California paper claiming that a baseball player had asked him to pay $50 for an autograph. Everyone was outraged and critical of this highly paid athlete. But the student was lying. The baseball player had never asked for the money. The boy lied in order to get the story printed. If this is the extent to which lying seems to be an accepted norm, and if this is what 12 year olds think is a way to get attention, what can we expect from our youth entering business? How can we hope that students will believe in the values being taught when they see business and government discrediting those same values. We cannot look to kids to assume responsibility until adults are appropriate role models. We will not have ethical role models until we accept the simplicity of right and wrong, and live accordingly.

MISSION STATEMENT

Corporate mission statements reveal a company's values and ethics. They can become an effective tool to implement change. They ensure that all employees understand the goals of the corporation. A recent study in *Say It and Live It* by Jones and Kahaner showed that managers used mission statements to help them through difficult times. These statements can become the operational, financial, and ethical guides for a business. A mission statement needs to be a well planned agreement on the vision of the corporation, the way to treat employees, and the ideals and values of a corporation. They can show us the human side of an entity. If business is to implement an ethical standard, the mission statement is the place to begin.

Many companies today have such statements and some actually seem to be following them. These declarations, however, are only a tool to assist in reestablishing trust, and obviously not a determining factor. The challenge is to prove with actions, not words. Companies must be willing not only to openly state their values, but also to enforce compliance of those values. This procedure becomes the responsibility of employees as well as employers. An important first step is putting the goals and values of a corporation in writing so managers, workers, and customers know what they are. A condition of a successful company is that those principles are also enacted within that corporation.

Trust is confidence in the honesty, reliability, integrity, and justice of an organization or person. The responsibility of business owners is to establish, with the help of managers and other employees, the accepted standards. Only this commitment and consistency will begin to affect the current situation. What we need to change is the fact that we are not doing what we should be doing. We have become lost in a philosophical debate to cover up the obvious. The answer is to begin acting on our basic and simple beliefs, such as honoring what is right and not allowing what is wrong.

SPIRITUALITY

Spirituality is the larger picture of the ethics issue that must be addressed. Any discussion on spirituality, especially in relation to business, is difficult since there are many strong feelings on the subject. If we can separate religion and spirituality, then the discussion becomes less volatile. This is not about religion. This is about the values that transcend any particular religion, the values most of us agree on. Until recently, any such discussion did not belong in a business context. We can no longer do things the old way. We must begin to allow some discussion of spirituality in our corporate world.

The industrial era provided a context in which we no longer needed to trust a Creator since we could trust science to explain our physical world. Humans were all important because we had conquered the universe through our science which could answer all questions about the physical world. In the beginning of the 20th century, we learned that we did not have all of the answers. Einstein and the quantum physicists showed us that the physical universe, both large and small, was much more complex and confusing than Newton's physics had led us to believe. As the century progressed, as the industrial era faded, and as the information era came of age, we once again needed something to believe in, something to replace the science that had seemingly displaced our earlier belief in a Supreme Being.

We can't go back to the same beliefs we had before science took us on a new path. We are wiser, more skeptical, and more cynical. The world has become more demanding and we do not like much of what we see. Not only do we not trust our corporations, organizations, others or ourselves, we no longer trust our Creator. How could a Creator allow such destruction to people and the environment? We lost faith in a spiritual power to ultimately lead us or the world to a better life.

The word that makes people even more uncomfortable than the word "spirituality" is the word "God." When I decided to write this book, most advice was to avoid using God as it might be too controversial in a business setting. I contend God is very controversial even in most social settings, which only reinforces our organizational dilemma. How do we simplify this problem? One way is to look at the facts. In a study reported in, *A Generation of Seekers: Spiritual Journey of Baby Boomers* by Wade, 95% of the people surveyed said that they believed in God. Another survey in a December 1994, *USA Weekend* article, reported that 9 out of 10 of us pray. So, most Americans believe in God.

In this time of the global village, we must be aware that not all world religions believe in a God. The Buddhists, for example, have a philosophy that does not include the term God. The problem with using the words God or Deity or Supreme Being is that they seem to exclude one or another group of people. In this age of diversity, we need to attempt to include as many people as possible. But we also need to honor our differences.

The significance to spirituality is that it is a belief in something greater than ourselves, a belief in a bigger picture. What we name this "greater than" is insignificant. What is important is that we each identify our beliefs, accept them, and use them as our standard for living. If one is brought up in the Christian or Jewish tradition, then "God" is an appropriate term. If one is a Buddhist or adheres to one of the many other religious philosophies, then other terms such as Nirvana are applicable. The differences in what these represent can remain unique to that group. The similarities are the bond that allows us to tolerate and interact with one another.

As soon as we attempt to define a Greater Being, we are at a loss since one cannot define an infinite concept with finite words. If we allow individuals or groups to use whatever deity term works for them, then we have arrived at a level of tolerance. More significant than a name are the concepts represented by that name. Whether a deity represents the highest good, right action, oneness with nature, oneness with others, or a combination of all of these, the similarities must be stressed. There are some general principles that seem to be common in religions worldwide. Most religions and spiritual paths teach principles of compassion, unity, truthfulness, fairness, tolerance, responsibility, respect for, and service to, all life. With these basic concepts as universal, how unfortunate that there is so much religious strife in the world. If we could only learn to act on our common beliefs, as opposed to dissecting and defending them.

MY STORY—SUICIDE

When life runs smoothly it is easy to avoid dealing with spirituality. When life falls apart, it is impossible to do so. My arrest and subsequent court experiences caused my world to fall apart. But even before I had faced the fateful outcome of my case, something occurred that further forced me to question life and search for new answers.

My sister called from Connecticut to tell me that our 23 year old niece, my brother's daughter, had tried to kill herself and was in a coma at the hospital with little chance of survival. She died two days later.

Shannon had first tried to commit suicide at age 13. At 23, she succeeded. Any death is difficult. Any close death is unbearable. Suicide adds another dimension. I accept her decision as right for her. I am learning not to judge another's actions. But the pain of it lingers. How do we justify the fact that life is so awful at age 23 that one is willing to leave? At that age I thought I was going to change the world. I set my goals and achieved them. I graduated from college, got married, bought a home, taught in high school, and studied for my master's degree. Nothing could stop me. What had stopped her? Why was her pain so bad ? Was this an isolated incident, or was life so different twenty years later?

Shannon was a troubled kid. Even though she was wise for her age, there was a part of her that had never grown beyond the 13 year old. Her family and society failed to help her through out those 10 years. What happened? Why couldn't any of us answer this youngster who was crying out? I don't know. The question haunts me. We all tried to assist—family, counselors, psychiatrists, and those at the mental health institute where she stayed for a while. Why are we at a loss as a society to help such troubled kids? The suicide rate among teenagers is high and it is rising. What is happening? I have trouble understanding an environment that forces, allows, or in some way seems to encourage such an answer. I blame no one, but I blame us all, all of society. We need to wake up to the consequences of troubled kids in a troubled world.

Death is an unspoken, scary topic until we are faced with it in a personal way. Then we grope unknowingly, with no skills to cope with the emotions. Suicide takes us a step further into the darkness. Not just death, but a conscious choice of death. This is even more difficult to understand.

A friend of mine was particularly helpful during my mourning. Dustin gave me permission to grieve and to feel the pain. She said it would take as long as necessary to get over the pain. An ambiguous, but accurate statement. Feel the emotions, this is the part we have lost. We have worked hard in our society to cover up the hurt. "Get back to work and it will be better," is often the advice. Yes, but in doing that, we forgot to allow the reality of the emotions.

As selfish as it may be, suicide is tough on those left. There is some guilt, but there is much more. Suicide forces us to look at our lives and come up with a meaningful answer. Shannon, the girl who seemed so alone, had many friends attend her funeral. These kids were deeply touched and they hurt. They needed answers. My heart went out to them. At 23, there are few life experiences to understand suicide. I realized I was incapable of consoling them. I was having too hard a time groping with my own disbelief and sorrow. I remember being annoyed at the church service. It was so impersonal, so out of touch. I wanted the priest to talk to those kids sitting there in pain for the loss of their friend. I wanted him to explain the death to them, to address their concerns, to assure them that suicide was not an answer. But this seemed beyond his capability. I expected something the church had never really provided for me—comfort. I hurt for those young adults, but my pain was as ineffective in helping them as was the priest's lack of words.

Suicide is lonely. I can't imagine how it must feel for the person taking a life. How lonely for the survivors. Lonely because there are no answers. Lonely because suicide stares at us, daring us to be at peace. Suicide is unsettling; forcing us to confront our own lives. I had to honor the incident and let it mean something.

In dealing with the aftermath of my court ordeal, suicide was one of my possible answers. I'm not sure I could have acted on my thoughts, but I do know there were times when I did not wish to continue this life. The concept of suicide is no longer scary, mainly because I have allowed myself the freedom of thinking and feeling. The worse thing we do with emotions is refuse to honor and acknowledge them. Allowing myself to say, "I'm thinking I may not want to live," was allowing myself to be honest, even though it seemed forbidden. If we would allow expression of our feelings, we could say to friends, "I'm thinking of suicide" and they would know to listen, and not panic or immediately try to get us to a psychiatrist. Death itself is not so scary, but the darkness of the thoughts frightens us. These are the musings that we're "not suppose to have." The fact is that we do have these questionings and we need an outlet for expressing them.

We are like little kids who know we are not allowed in a certain room, yet sneak in to see why we're not allowed. Most often, the room is not so interesting or scary. We need to rebel against the denied access to some of our emotions, the dark side. If we begin to honor our emotions, we have to feel the pain and sorrow as well as the joy and happiness. We must not be afraid to look at death.

We must confront the potential of nothingness, the fear of losing our self. The pain of that potential loss is real because no one prepares us for this thing called death.

Expressing my suicidal thoughts made the blackness of suicide and death less awesome and less powerful. Suicide lost its power when I gave myself permission to look at it as a possible option, and then it no longer became a wanted option. My confrontation released me to look at what my life meant and why I might choose to live. I have always read that looking into the abyss was necessary in order to go forward. But that was an intellectual statement, not an emotional understanding. I have now looked into that abyss and know that it is not so scary, because I found something there.

We all need to find something more to life, a bigger picture, a reason to care, a reason to go on, and a reason to help others. These are only some of the issues each of us must answer for ourselves. Our answers become our spirituality, our view of life. Perhaps if we could find such answers, we would have more fulfilled, less scary lives, and maybe we could even begin to help ourselves as well as our troubled youth.

TRUSTING A SPIRITUAL BASE

Our current belief in a Creator does not translate to choosing between right and wrong in our lives or in business, and our current belief does not seem to translate to a better life for us. We know "something is missing," but we are afraid to trust a deity that has seemingly let us down. Reestablishing our trust in a Greater Being or Power is necessary. Without this trust, there is a void. We know it, but we have felt helpless in deciding what to do. The answer can be simple. Begin to trust again in a Creator, just as we must trust in ourselves and others. Remember that we never lost our belief. Our beliefs have always been with us on some level. Trusting in that belief is what we lost.

Religion should provide answers. But organized religion has become, in many instances, a set of dogmatic doctrines forced upon individuals who are expected to blindly, and without question, accept them. Organized religion is one of the institutions that is no longer working and fits in the category of nonfunctioning organizations. There are some exceptions, just as there are some very progressive and successfully run corporations and schools. But most religions as they are practiced today do not belong in business. Spirituality, however, must be a part of business. Our challenge is to be smarter about the distinction.

The Native Americans offer us much wisdom in their simplistic beliefs. They teach that we should have a balance in the four aspects of life: spiritual, physical, emotional or social, and intellectual. We must return to the values that have withstood time. We need to step back and remind ourselves about those things which we know are right, those things that are hidden in our inner knowing, that deep internal wisdom. A favorite quotation from Hermann Hesse, the German author, states that:

Within you there is a stillness and sanctuary to which you can retreat at any time and be yourself.

Perhaps it is time for us to retreat to our sanctuary since the world has gotten too confusing. In this stillness we meet our spirituality, and we know and choose the correct action for our lives. If we can learn to do this and then bring that wisdom into our business, integrity will return.

PART III

IMPLEMENTING TRUST IN THE WORKPLACE

Businesses must become the leaders of change; I see little hope in governmental decrees. We learn from political parties that words, no matter how powerful, become meaningless as commitments made are soon broken. Both parties, pressured with changing times, are spending too much energy on blame instead of working together to solve the problems that are not exclusively the fault of either party. Rather the fault is in a system gone awry, a product of the times. The government represents the best example of an organization not working, a macrocosm of what occurs in many corporations. The government represents a societal ill.

Business leaders are led by economic restraints and rewards to function in the most effective way. Because of this, economics is our greatest hope. We no longer trust words. Positive actions are the only answer.

We must reinstate a sense of trust. Chapter 7 provides practical exercises to assess and implement the new ideas. Chapter 8 provides additional suggestions for executing the necessary transformations. Activities in both chapters apply to individuals and companies as well as to business owners.

7

ENTREPRENEURIAL THINKING

SOCIALLY CONSCIOUS WORKERS AND COMPANIES

Chapter 1 discusses abundance and the importance of the worker as two ideas spawned by computers. Chapter 2 shows the understanding of change that is beginning to dominate our lives, and Chapter 3 presents the social awareness that money is no longer the only definition of success. Chapter 4 deals with trusting ourselves and our emotions. Chapter 5 talks of trusting others and accepting diversity, and Chapter 6 points out the need for an ethical standard. These concepts can be related to jobs and companies. They can be used to assess which values are important to you and which ones are espoused by your company.

Exercise 1 should be done in two stages. First, go through the questions and determine which of the items you consider important in a business. In answering, think in terms of your own feelings. Trust your own instincts. Answer based on how you feel things should be, not on how you know they are, or how society has trained you to think. Rate yourself and determine your score. Second, go through the same questions and rate your company. Be honest and as accurate as possible in the assessment.

There may be disagreements concerning the significance of the twelve questions. View them in relation to a new way of thinking based on the ideas presented in this book. Do not attempt to look at them through the eyes of a 20th century industrial age individual. Try to become the 21st century knowledge individual. Some of the ideas are obvious, some may seem unrealistic. Yet each of them represents a departure from the business environment that allowed the demise of trust and each of them represents a move toward a new professional climate.

EXERCISE 1

ASSESSING SOCIALLY CONSCIOUS WORKERS AND COMPANIES

Directions:
First, rate yourself based on which statements you feel are important in a business. Second, do the same exercise and rate the company you work for.

1. Your company has a Mission Statement (1 point):
   A. stating the vision and values, or ethics, of the company (1 point),
   B. developed with input from owner, managers and worker (1 point), and
   C. that is enforced or honored within the company (1 point).

2. Your company provides the following:
   A. flexible time in addition to family leave for mothers and fathers (2 points), and
   B. child care or child care provisions, if appropriate (2 points).

3. Your company:
   A. has a stated policy against bias based on gender, race, sexual preference, or any other determinant (2 points), and
   B. honors, or enforces, its antidiscrimination policy (2 points).

4. Your company provides honest and truthful information about products being sold to customers (4 points).

5. Your company charges a fair mark-up on its products or "services". The profit is reasonable, considering the risk and the market, not excessive (4 points).

6. Your company's overhead is relatively low or sensible, based on what is a reasonable budget for the particular industry (4 points).

7. Your company offers good benefits, such as health, vacation, sick leave, and educational opportunities, based on what is reasonable for the industry and the particular company (4 points).

8. There is an effort within your company to:
   A. help workers advance to higher positions and to encourage promotions (2 points), and
   B. promote personal responsibility for each worker (2 points).

9. Officers and owners make only a set amount more than workers, such as the president makes 10 or 20 times more than the lowest paid workers (4 points).

10. Workers are encouraged and rewarded with bonuses, ESOP (employee stock option plans), and/or some participation in profits (4 points).

11. Your company has a concern for the environment with:
    A. a recycling policy (2 points), and
    B. efforts made to be sure there is no toxic, or other serious, pollution (2 points).

12. Your company takes an active role in helping the local community, not just a passive role of giving money. An active role might involve encouraging employees to help build homes for the homeless, or provide education to a deserving group (4 points).

Scoring: Highest Possible Score is 48 points

1. Add the points to determine your score. A score of 40 or better shows a socially conscious worker.

2. Add the points to determine the score for your company. A score of 40 or better shows a socially conscious company.

3. Do you and your company have similar scores? If not, where is the discrepancy? If the company rates very low and you rate very high, what are you doing about the discrepancies? Is there some action you can take to remedy the situation. If not, what are your options? What do you intend to do about the differences?

Each of the questions in **Exercise 1** is addressed in previous chapters. If you find yourself disagreeing with an item, look at the idea behind the question. Below is a list of the concepts and the chapters in which they are discussed.

Question 1	Ethical Standard	Chapter 6
Question 2	Importance of Worker	Chapter 1
Question 3	Diversity	Chapter 5
Question 4	Honesty	Chapter 6
Question 5	Abundance	Chapter 1
Question 6	Definition of Success	Chapter 3
Question 7	Importance of Worker	Chapter 1
Question 8	Importance of Worker	Chapter 1
Question 9	Abundance	Chapter 1
Question 10	Abundance	Chapter 1
Question 11	Social Awareness	Chapter 3
Question 12	Social Awareness	Chapter 3

ENTREPRENEURIAL THINKING

With so many people losing jobs, we are seeing an increase in the number of people starting their own companies. They are the "reluctant entrepreneurs", starting their own ventures or going to work for small firms because of lack of other opportunities or because of frustration with large corporations.

John Naisbitt, in his book *Global Paradox,* states that the entrepreneur is the most important player in the new global economy. Small businesses are the key to future success. Entrepreneurs are more adaptable and do not have big profits from past years as a cushion. Only companies that are willing to change will thrive. Some larger corporations, those willing to shift significantly, will help lead the way. Others will simply rely on the "government mentality" of blame and useless struggle to maintain some semblance of the status quo. Small companies who understand the changes will become the leaders. Big is not the only answer. "Grow or die," a term used to describe business, needs to be reassessed. Growing in quality and effectiveness may redefine growing in size. The old ways must give way to a new view. Every previously accepted concept should be subject to scrutiny, with little tolerance for "but this is the way it has always been done."

Entrepreneurship promotes not only owning one's own business, but also taking control of one's life by making ideas happen. Within a corporation, the term "intrapreneurship" is used to describe individuals showing initiative and an independence.

Chapter 2 presented the new scientific theory of chaos in which complex organisms, or individuals and organizations, are described as "bounded instability." This refers to the fact that there is an intricate mix of order and disorder. An acceptance of instability as a natural and continual occurrence within business is a challenge. This instability means that long-term planning is very difficult since the future is unknowable. There is a need to view business from an entrepreneurial framework which encourages adaptability and handling chaotic conditions.

Creativity and risk are entrepreneurial characteristics. After being in business for a few years, I understand that creativity is not just about painting a picture, acting in a drama, writing a novel or some other artistic endeavor. Creativity is being intellectually inventive. Successful business people must be imaginative and innovative. In adapting to change, a larger view of creativity is necessary. Risk is a part of creativity. We must be willing to try new ideas, new ways of doing things. This involves a certain degree of risk. Venturing into the unknown is both creative and risky and the chaos theory suggests that the unknown is a reality for our future.

An additional aspect of the chaos theory, as explained in Chapter 2, is non-linear thinking in which there is no one cause and effect, making predictions even more difficult. Non-linear is a new way of thinking. The world hasn't changed, but our way of viewing it has shifted. We can no longer expect to find one cause for an event, or expect an outcome to have a single, definite cause. Talk of the "information highway" is misleading since it implies linear thinking, or moving in a straight line. Instead think in terms of a web of ideas spreading out in a variety of intricate patterns, but with an underlying order.

The term "entrepreneurial thinking" refers to non-linear thinking, as opposed to the stricter definition of someone starting or running a small business. How do we define this "entrepreneurial thinking?" Exercise 2 provides some of the common entrepreneurial characteristics. First, use the Exercise to assess yourself as an entrepreneurial thinker and then follow the same procedure to assess your company. Do you have the qualities necessary to adapt to changes as they will occur in business? Does your business exhibit the appropriate adaptive qualities? These qualities indicate a beginning of non-linear thinking. If none of the qualities apply, what can you do to promote some new type of thinking within your own work environment?

EXERCISE 2

ARE YOU AN ENTREPRENEURIAL THINKER?

Directions:
1. Assign one point for each characteristic that describes, or mostly describes you.
2. Assign one point for each characteristic that describes your immediate supervisor, if applicable.
3. Assign one point for each characteristic that applies to your company.

An Entrepreneurial Thinker:

Creates or seizes an opportunity and pursues it regardless of current resources.

Never, never accepts "no" for an answer

Is creative and innovative, but has solid management and business skills

Uses both left and right brain

Works hard, is driven by intense commitment and determined perseverance

Sees the cup 1/2 full, not 1/2 empty

Strives for integrity

Burns with competitive desire to excel

Is dissatisfied with the status quo

Seeks opportunity to improve any situation

Uses failure as a learning tool

Strives for effectiveness, not perfection

Is comfortable with a certain degree of risk

Scoring: Highest Possible Score is 13

A score of 10 or more makes you, your supervisor and/or your company an entrepreneurial thinker.

If your score is low, decide if you agree that these characteristics are valuable ones for you to achieve. If so, what can you do to act more entrepreneurial?

If your score is significantly higher than your supervisor's or your firm's, do you see some hope for change? Do you need to reevaluate your job, or are you confident that the company will be successful in the future despite the lack of these traits?

MANAGERIAL RESPONSIBILITIES

Bounded instability provides the comfort that there is order in the bigger picture. We can trust that even in a chaotic situation, a new order will arise. This means that tension is normal. In addition to entrepreneurial thinking, a new view of management is necessary to cope with this tension. We need to see managing ourselves, our lives, our jobs, our employees, and our companies in a different light. One view is that there are three main responsibilities, or main areas, of management: Think, Decide and Do.[32] These apply to our lives and our jobs as well as all levels of managing.

THINK—This is the area of planning. This area is often neglected when the immediate pressures of life become too demanding. This area must be given time on a routine basis in order to deal with the inevitable changes. The amount of time will vary with each company and each situation. The new strategic planning is a brainstorming session of option development in which possibilities and their probability are assessed and debated. This creative process involves as many of the players within a business as possible. Managerial thinking is not limited to managers. Anyone who has input, or knowledge regarding a process, product, or service being discussed, should participate.

DECIDE—This is the area of assessing the options developed in the thinking process, and choosing the most appropriate course of action. Sometimes a decision is made to make no changes. But this in itself is a decision. With instability inherent in the computer age, businesses need to be capable of quick decisions. Making these decisions is easier when possible options are already available.

DO—This is the area of implementing the decisions.

These three areas seem very simple, and they are. Yet, review your own life and your recent business decisions. How much concerted time was spent in the three processes? Each is a valid and distinct function; each is separate activity. Too often we lump them into one. They may, in fact, be done by only one individual, as when we make a personal decision, or the boss makes a unilateral business determination. But even within an individual, there are the three distinct processes. One must determine the options, assess the options to determine the best one for the situation, and then act on that decision.

The most important aspect of this managerial responsibility view is that it gives credence to the thinking phase. Too often we neglect this phase or forget to honor it as important. When was the last time that you felt good at the end of a day or period of time during which you simply "thought" about the future or some problem. We tend to assume that time spent thinking is wasted or unproductive. Thinking isn't easily measured. Yet without this process, no valid decisions for the future can be made and no improvement in the implementation phase occurs.

We seem to have perfected the process of "doing." We can measure our output and feel satisfied that we accomplished something. Neither Thinking nor Deciding carry the same weight. Without time spent on all three responsibilities, a company will not continue to advance. The pressure of business today tends to force too many of us into surviving. The only way to advance into the 21st century is to give time and credence to all areas of managerial thinking. If we accept the concept of change impinging upon our lives, we must move into an adaptive mode of advancing.

EXERCISE 3

MANAGERIAL RESPONSIBILITIES

Directions:
1. Do each activity for yourself in relation to your job.
2. Do each activity for your company.

I. Thinking, Deciding, and Doing
Answer the questions and fill out the Chart below.

A. What amount of time in your job is spent on planning? This applies to everyone, even if you are in a secure job, or think you are. Include the time you spend on planning for the future and for any obsolescence, such as attending strategic meetings, reading about new advances in your industry, or assessing the impact of new discoveries.

B. How many hours are spent assessing options proposed in the Thinking process? This includes time spent eliminating the options not valid now. Count time spent deciding, even if it is time deciding not do anything.

C. How many hours are spent on implementing, or doing the job? This period would be the bulk of time for each of us.

This activity should be based on the average number of hours a month that you work. It is not important to be too detailed. Rough estimates work.
When answering questions in relation to your company, estimate the overall number of hours per month spent on each responsibility.

Responsibility	Hours	Percentage of Time
Thinking (developing options) _____		_____
Deciding (choosing options) _____		_____
Doing (implementing decisions)_____		_____
Total Hours/Percentage		100%

II. Advancing or Surviving

Advancing defines spending time preparing for changes
(Thinking and Deciding).
Surviving defines spending time doing the focus of your business
(Doing).

Assess what percentage of time in a month is spent on each activity.
The answer will differ with each individual person and company.

What is the percentage of time moving forward
(Thinking and Deciding)—**Advancing**_____

What is the percentage of time maintaining
(Doing)—**Surviving** _____

Scoring: A score of 15-30% on Advancing is an acceptable range.

1. If both you and your company spend at least 15% of the time Advancing, keep up the good work.

2. If there is less than 15% of your time in Advancing, you should consider revisiting your priorities.

3. If both you and company rate below 15% of time on Advancing, what steps are you going to take to change the situation?

4. If you or your company spend over 30% of your time on Advancing (and your job is not at a think tank), you or your company might want to stop thinking and get to work.

5. If you spend between 15-30% of your time on Advancing but your company does not, are you planning to move to a more adaptive company?

EXERCISE 4

WHAT IS YOUR PASSION?

I. There is an important question referring to your job:
Does it matter?[33]

Whatever your job, is there something about it that you feel is important? The key words here are, "you feel." This is not a question about what others might think about your job. This is an honest, personal assessment. Does it matter, is it important? Does the overall view of your job make you feel that you are contributing something to help make the world better in some small or big way. Be realistic, not idealistic in your answers. Making toilet paper is important, making pencils is important and serving food in a restaurant is important to the people eating in that restaurant. Don't make this a bigger question than it seems. It does not matter why you originally went into the business, such as it was the only job available at the time or you hated the industry but the money was good. The point is to assess your current feeling about it. So ask yourself again: Does what you do matter?
Yes_____   **No**_____

II. A. List 5 different identities or roles that you play in life, such as mother/father, wife/husband or other, sister/brother, resident of a particular state, American or other nationality, Catholic or some other religion, piano player or some other hobby, writer or whatever your job is, volunteer at some charity or other activity you participate in, or any other identity or role you play in your private or public life.

B. For each identity, write a short description that defines you in that role or defines your biggest concern about that role. As a mother, you may be most concerned about the education of your

kids. As a Catholic, you may be most concerned about the seemingly unfair divorce laws of the Church. As an American, you may
be most concerned about the taxes you pay or the lack of leadership
today. This activity should not take a lot of time. Consider the first
words that come to mind when you think of yourself in that role.
Simply write down the words for each identity.

C. Review your descriptions. These should indicate at least 5
subjects that you really care about—subjects that you are passionate
about. From this list, choose three words that might answer the following questions:

Where is your passion?
What keeps you awake at night?
What do you really believe in?

List three subjects that you are passionate about.
1._____
2._____
3._____

III. Choose one word that best describes who you are. Such words
as learner, fixer or laugher can define a significant aspect of your
personality. It is simply the one word that you feel best defines you,
whatever that is. Again, don't make this a major project or try to
search for some major significance. Just be honest and choose what
first comes to mind.

One word description_____

IV. Review the list of three subjects in II above and the one word
description in III above. These are the things you are passionate
about. Does your job provide the opportunity for you to act on, spend
time on, or otherwise relate to any of your passions?

Yes_____ **No**_____

JOB REQUIREMENTS AND STRENGTHS

In **Exercise 5,** you are asked to assess your weekly work activities. What are the activities that you spend the majority of your time doing? What consumes most of your time? What are you actually being paid for?

In **Exercise 6,** assess your strengths to see what you are good at, what you are not good at, and what you can improve upon. The goal is to concentrate on things which you are good at doing. This is not an excuse for avoiding jobs you don't like, rather a way for you and your company to utilize you and your talents in the most efficient way. The jobs you hate to do will be the ones you do least well and the ones you procrastinate doing.

EXERCISE 5

ACTIVITY-BASED ANALYSIS[34]

I. Gather Data

A. List each activity that you do weekly, being as specific as possible.

B. For each activity, list the amount of time you spend doing it.

C. For each activity, list the percentage of time you spend doing it.

Here is a sample chart based on only 5 activities. Your activities will vary considerably.

Example: Activity		Time	Percentage of Time
Activity 1	supervising	5 hours	12.5%
Activity 2	creative tasks	5 hours	12.5%
Activity 3	meetings	10 hours	25%
Activity 4	returning phone calls	10 hours	25%
Activity 5	paperwork	10 hours	25%
Total		40 hours	100%

Use this chart to fill in your activities and time. For this Exercise, choose the 10 most time-consuming activities that you do weekly.

Activity	Time	Percentage
Activity 1		
Activity 2		
Activity 3		
Activity 4		
Activity 5		
Activity 6		
Activity 7		
Activity 8		
Activity 9		
Activity 10		
Total		100%

II. Analyze Data

List the three activities that you spend most of your time doing.

1._____

2._____

3._____

EXERCISE 6

A FOUR-STEP METHOD OF ASSESSING YOUR WORK3[5]

I. ASSESS yourself in relation to your job:

Assess your strengths—what you do well.
Assess your weakness—what you do not do well.
Assess partial successes—what do you do half well

In assessing your strengths, weaknesses, and partial successes, refer back to **Exercise 5, Activity-Based Analysis**. Be honest, this is only for yourself. Assess the situation as it is, not as you wish it were.

Example (refers back to Exercise 5 on previous page):

Strengths	Weaknesses	Partial Successes
Activity 1—supervising	Activity 5—paperwork	Activity 3—meetings
Activity 2—creative tasks		Activity 4— returning phone calls

Use the chart on the following page to fill in your activities from **Exercise 5**.

Strengths	Weaknesses	Partial Successes
_____	_____	_____
_____	_____	_____
_____	_____	_____
_____	_____	_____

II. ANALYZE each category. Determine if your strengths are in one particular activity, or if your strengths vary. Do your strengths relate to the actual activities you spend most of your time doing, or are you spending most of your time doing activities in which you are not most effective?

III. ABANDON what you do not do well. Decide how to eliminate the things you don't do well. Can the jobs be given to someone else? Could they be outsourced? If you don't do them well, would it benefit you and the company to have someone else do them?

IV. ASPIRE to cut out, or change, jobs you do only half well. Decide how to either eliminate these partial successes, or work on improving them so you can move them to your strengths area.

IV. CONCENTRATE on what you do well.

Concentrate on those activities that are your strengths

Scoring:

1. How many of the activities listed in **Exercise 5, Activity-Based Analysis** are in the Strengths column? If at least 6 of the 10 are strengths, congratulations on having a job fitting your talents!

2. If there are fewer than 3 activities that are strengths, what are you doing to change your daily activities?

3. Have you figured out a way to eliminate some of the activities listed in your Weakness column?

4. Have you devised a plan to improve upon the activities in your Partial Success column?

5. Refer back to **Exercise 4, What is Your Passion?** Determine if the activities that you list as your strengths are also the activities that are related at all to what you feel strongly about. Are you spending time doing what is important to you?
   Yes_____ **No**_____

In reviewing Chapter 7, ask the following questions:

1. If you aren't socially conscious, how can you be trusted to treat others with integrity?

2. If you don't display some of the entrepreneurial thinking characteristics, how can you be trusted to help your company meet the challenges of tomorrow?

3. If you don't value thinking and deciding as important, how can you be trusted to make well-thought out decisions?

4. If you don't feel your job is important, how can you be trusted to do it well?

5. If your job doesn't relate to anything that you are passionate about, how can you be trusted to give your job as much energy as you give your interests or hobbies?

6. If you are not working in areas that reflect your strengths, how can you be trusted to do the best job possible?

Questions 1-6 relate to you as an individual.
Questions 7-12 relate to your company.

7. If your company isn't socially conscious, how can you trust it to treat you with integrity and respect?

8. If your company doesn't encourage entrepreneurial thinking, how can you trust it will successfully meet the challenges of tomorrow?

9. If your company doesn't value thinking and deciding, how can you trust it to make the best decisions?

10. If your company doesn't think your job is important, how can you trust that supervisors will care how well you perform?

11. If your company doesn't represent any of your passions, how can you expect it to ever meet your expectations?

12. If your company doesn't encourage you to work in areas of your strength, how can you trust it to fairly evaluate you?

8

INTERDEPENDENCE

INTERDEPENDENCE

One of my mentors once told me that the most important thing in life is to ask the right questions. It was a useful piece of advice that applies in most situations. At the end of Chapter 7 there are significant questions that must be asked of ourselves and our corporations in relation to trust. That chapter shows that we need to be very clear which principles are important to us in order to be sure our companies represent those same values. Chapter 8 continues the quest for ways to implement trust in our businesses.

There is a series of steps to promote trust within an organization. Hiring the right people or choosing the right company is important. Training new and existing employees in order to be assured that all understand the required skills is another step. Once expectations are stated, it is necessary to set up an accountability system to assure the requirements will be enforced. The last step is to set up a reward system that is equitable and encourages the principles deemed important.

Interdependence consists of decentralization and giving up control. If, in fact, there is a belief in the significance of change in our businesses, and a belief that people are once again important, then decentralization is one answer. This allows individuals to adapt quickly to the necessary changes as a result of external or internal forces. Large corporations have become flawed with their cumbersome bureaucratic procedures. Without these same constraints, smaller groups can function more easily, an entrepreneurial trait.

Smaller groups within a larger organization are useless unless they have the authority to make decisions. This is often the hardest part of the equation since allowing subordinates to actually function in a managerial capacity seems too scary. The whole process comes full circle when we realize that if we could trust the skills of subordinates, we could allow the process to work. Letting go of control can only be done in the context of hiring the right people, training the existing people, insisting on accountability for actions, and rewarding results.

HIRING

If we say trust is important, then we must include it in our hiring process. The interview is a time for the potential employer and employee to assess one another. It is not a one-sided interrogation. If this process can be refined to meet the expectations of each side, managers will find life easier. Defining the exact required criteria is the only way to assure success.

My sister has owned a recruitment agency in Connecticut for over 10 years.[36] In the past 5 years, she has seen a shift in the hiring process from simple competence requirements to reliance on personal, subjective concerns. This change reflects downsizing, with fewer employees doing the same amount of work. The change also requires a versatile worker with more than one skill set. Since employees need to do multiple jobs, they also need to interact with each other. Even technical workers must be social as they work on teams. All of this reinforces the importance of trust among workers. Stephen R. Covey in *First Things First* talks of hiring people with character as well as competence. If we want to hire people with character, then we need to look at whether or not the person exhibits qualities of integrity.

Workers who adapt easily and are entrepreneurial thinkers are also essential in today's environment. This is discussed in Chapter 7 and addressed in Exercise 2, Entrepreneurial Thinking. This same exercise can be used as part of the interview process. Other qualities in Chapter 7 are important in the hiring process if trust is to be encouraged. Employees and employers must:

1. reflect the same principles
2. care about their jobs
3. feel their job matters
4. care about others
5. know their own areas of strength
6. believe in abundance for all within a company
7. exhibit a tolerance of diversity

If a company is clear about its concepts of trust and those goals are clearly stated, then it is a simple matter to determine if an individual fits in. If the company clearly presents its views, the individual can easily make an informed decision.

TRAINING

Hiring is one aspect of assuring trustworthy employees. But what about the current employees? Expecting different behavior from any group requires training. But this training cannot be a one-way street. It is not solely the responsibility of the employer to train the employee. Understanding the ideas presented throughout this book must be the duty of the individual. Employees must rely on themselves, not on the corporation to take care of their future.

Education is a continual process. The employer is responsible for informing employees about the latest changes within the firm. The employee is responsible for knowing the current industry trends. This education can be simply reading industry magazines; it does not need to be formal training. With access to the Internet, anyone can find appropriate information. Without this individual effort of keeping abreast of new developments, workers have no right to complain about their jobs becoming obsolete or changed. The discernible and informed employer and employee will recognize trends and be prepared for the future.

A reminder about training is that a one or two day seminar does not turn a business or its people around. Patience is required. Any attempt instituted by decree will not work. Let us learn from past failures.

Assessment

Do not attempt to make changes without a clear understanding of what is already working and what needs to be changed. Any training, any new idea, any new concept must be tailored to a particular situation of a particular company. The "one size fits all" does not work any more. Employees, managers, and owners alike are leery of the latest fad. Any effective training must take into account the attitudes, beliefs, and concerns of the current work force.

There are many assessment tools. They can be purchased or devised in-house. The process need not be difficult or time-consuming. One effective method is to simply ask the employees about their concerns. In this technological era, we have worked hard to create a complicated world of figures and numbers to assure control of all situations. The individual and the simple solution get lost in this maze. Ask the employees and they will tell you what isn't working, what their concerns are, and what training would be most effective. Poll the owners, managers, and workers. Ask everyone, listen to their answers, and act on their advice.

Training must start with an assessment to set up objectives that are clearly defined. Know what is expected from the training before it begins. This is true with all types of education, but it is especially true in the softer area of people skills and fairness. There are 12 main concepts that must be present if a firm wants to be assured that trust will exist and be encouraged:

1. Abundance mentality
2. Recognition of the importance of individual workers
3. Change as a natural part of business
4. Adaptability
5. Understanding that success is not defined solely in terms of money
6. Cooperation, not competition
7. Self-esteem
8. Accepting the negative as well as positive aspects of individuals
9. Diversity
10. Communication
11. Honesty
12. Belief in a spiritual base

Which ones are most important for your firm? Which ones already exist? Which ones need improving? The answers to these questions will provide a starting point for your training.

Teams

Teams have become the new way to do business; they are one of the latest fads in industry. As such, they might require little time or energy. But teams represent a larger concept and this larger concept must be continually addressed. Teams require that people work well together, interdependence in action. Most of us do not come out of the womb with a good understanding of how to work well with others. Yet the skill can be learned. One of the strengths I notice at Anderson Schools of Management at the University of New Mexico is that students are required to work in teams. By the time these business students graduate, they are very proficient at group interaction and formal presentations. Don't expect employees to automatically have these skills, however. If teams aren't working, there is a reason. That reason needs to be addressed. Most often, simply providing some direction in the functioning of a good team will work. Simple requirements for effective teams include:

1. A goal
The group needs to have a clear direction, one understood by everyone in the group.

2. A group leader
This leader may change from project to project. But each specific task needs a designated individual to be sure the group is on track and objectives are being met. Consensual agreement is theoretically desirable, but not always practical. While a group may strive for such understanding, someone needs to have the authority to make decisions in case of disagreements or deadlocks.

3. Accountability
The group needs to have clear objectives on how to reach the final goal. This includes an agreed upon timeline and a clearly defined measurement of results. Measuring does not necessarily mean numerical accountability. It may just mean that a workable decision must be reached. Every group member must understand the desired end product.

4. Consequences to actions
As part of accountability, there must be consequences if

deadlines are not met or objectives not achieved. These can be any variety of actions accepted at a particular company. Group action becomes wasted energy without a compelling reason to achieve results.

These characteristics apply to any group interaction. Employees will not learn to trust employers and other employees until they learn how to work together.

Communication

Communication is the most important element in training. As with teamwork, this skill in not necessarily an inherent quality. Interaction within an organization can be improved if individuals learn to listen. One method is described in the Communication section of Chapter 5. Diversity in the workplace is an integral part of any organization for the 21st century and will only be successful with understanding one another and a mutual respect.

Communication is repeatedly mentioned in business literature and news reports as one of the most important skills for success. Reading and writing, as well as speaking and listening, must be part of our educational process, especially with the emphasis on email and computer transactions. We assume that people know how to transact business with email and other interactive methods. But understanding one another in words over the computer is a challenge, and one that requires some instruction.

ACCOUNTABILITY

Accountability is the step after training. There is a major trust issue in relation to accountability. Employees stopped believing they were being fairly evaluated as bottom line results dominated our businesses. Measuring concrete results in manufacturing, sales and profitability is easy. Measuring improved internal relations is more difficult. We have few reliable and acceptable instruments to assess non-numerical results. This is a major concern for most human resource people who see their jobs threatened with downsizing . Even though the human resource area is acknowledged as important, it has not been directly related to the bottom line and is too often deemed expendable. The dilemma becomes stronger as the need arises to hire ever more qualified employees, ones with all the characteristics discussed in the Hiring section. The challenge is for human resource people to take charge of their destiny and create some accountability tools appropriate for their particular company and industry. Measuring is important in our cost effective businesses.

I wish I could suggest that I have a definitive answer to measuring the "soft" skills. I don't. But I do have some thoughts on how to begin addressing the issue, using education as an example. Business and education have much to learn from one another. Teachers are being forced into standardized testing that ignores much of what is important. Business leaders are forced into numerical standards to assess an area they acknowledge as important, but are at a loss to measure otherwise.

In 1976, I completed my doctorate thesis on assessing student responses to literature. As a literature teacher, I was attempting to measure how students felt about what they read. I believed then, as I still do, that how a student feels about what is read is as important as the factual understanding of the work. This same argument, with obvious variations, applies to our current predicament in business. How do we measure that employees work better together or have a better attitude about the company after a given period of time or a policy change? Even though we can just ask them, we need a way to objectively assess such a change. The continual dilemma is how to objectively measure subjective subjects. The final answer is beyond the scope of this book. But a look at what I discovered in measuring subjective feelings to literature is a beginning.

A process called "content analysis" measured the students' writing to determine which of the four types of responses, Judgment, Sympathy, Empathy, or Projection were exhibited.[37] The study showed that the process of content analysis, based on already established research, could measure emotional responses. Obviously, there would have to be major changes before any such process could be applied to a business setting. But enough work has been done to show that we can measure these seemingly nebulous areas. If we recognize the validity and spend a little time and energy, we can develop a workable measurement.

When I first suggested the topic of assessing emotional responses for my thesis, I was told by my advisors not to venture into such a difficult area. Only my stubborn persistence allowed me to proceed. I have less patience with this type of argument now, 20 years later. We know that there are areas we can change. We just need the conviction to do so. So I encourage all companies and all employees within those companies to know that there is a way to measure those areas that seem to defy accountability. The answers are usually simpler than we realize. Someone needs to encourage the process. Too often we get caught in the dominant thinking of "it can't be done" or "it isn't done." Go back to the argument about entrepreneurial thinking and never taking "no" for an answer. The first tries often need refinement, but there must be a beginning. The challenge is to find creative ways to fit trust into accountability.

REWARDS

In order to validate trust within a company, the reward system must mirror the words. Saying that workers are important or that abundance is embraced by the corporation becomes meaningless unless those words are backed by actions. These actions need to be different from the old procedures. If cooperation is encouraged, then basing promotions and bonuses on competitive standards doesn't work.

I have seen two methods of rewards, one dealing with customers and one dealing with employees that have been very effective. Each reflects a particular industry but has implications for all businesses.

Employee Specific Rewards

The first is a procedure introduced nationwide in supermarkets that addresses customers. I see the same concept viable for employees. The actual methods used are less important than the concepts behind them. They are usually called frequent shopper programs and are similar, but not identical, to the frequent flyer programs. Supermarkets realized that when they offered specials, customers would come in for that item but then return to their usual grocery store. The special didn't convert customers, it just encouraged one-time shoppers to take advantage of the sale. This system rewarded the infrequent customer as much as it rewarded the faithful and long-term shopper.

The idea behind the concept is to reward the loyal customer. This involves offering specials to customers who have a designated card. The newer idea, as explained in Brian Woolf's *Customer Specific Marketing,* is to reward the customer based on how much is purchased and eventually to offer rewards based on past purchases. Computers can track the buying trends of the best customers and reward them with coupons for products that they often buy, not specials on dog food when they don't own a dog. The specific needs of each customer are met, "customer specific marketing." Computers have opened up this possibility and provide the capability of identifying the buyers and their purchases. The program rewards customers in two ways. First, the program rewards them for the amount of business they do with a store by giving free or discounted merchandise to those who spend a designated amount of money over a certain period of time. Second, the program rewards customers with discounts on products they purchase frequently.

Customers should be treated as individuals, not as if "one size fits all." This is not a new concept. Many businesses give bigger discounts for more business. As usual, this is not a new idea as much as applying an older concept in a new way.

There are further implications to this type of program. But I am interested only in addressing the aspect that relates to trust. Most of this book has centered on the idea of trust between employer and employee. The same issues arise with our customers. Surveys show that trust is one of the biggest problems for customers. Price is not the only determining factor in purchasing. We prefer to do business with companies that we can depend on over the long term. Rewarding the best customers aims at this understanding.

Getting new clients is expensive. Yet our focus has been on getting the new, not taking care of the old. I learned that lesson in the brokerage business where it was much easier to work on retaining the current clients and getting more business from them, than putting too much energy into getting new clients. Both are valid. It is just that the focus became too strong toward the new. We lost sight of taking care of the established clients.

In talking with one of the supermarket chains using this program, I listened to how difficult it was to initially train the managers to accept the new program. The old way of thinking is so ingrained, that anything new is difficult to institute. This is a lesson in all that we do. Owners and operators must realize that no matter how great, the idea will not work until it is embraced by the employees. The long term approach must be used. Distrust crept in over the years. Trust will not return overnight. Programs such as customer specific marketing will take time.

This new type of marketing can work with employees. We all know how expensive it is to train new employees. In a time of downsizing and disappearing loyalty, instituting methods to reward employees differently may be one answer. Remunerating for past behavior gives employees confidence that they are appreciated. This encourages trust and loyalty. Compensating them with specific rewards that identify individual interest is the new element. Not everyone is motivated by money. For some, time off is the best prize. For others, recognition works best. Knowing individual employees and knowing what they would most appreciate is one variation of specific marketing. This is a concept worth pursuing.

Shared Commissions

A second way of rewarding employees is a logical consequence of interdependence. We talk of cooperation. Yet most of our reward methods are competitive. The top producer gets a bonus or the employee of the month gets a parking space. We need to keep individual motivation high and encourage individual participation. But we must rethink our processes. If we say teams are important, we must reward them. I visited an art gallery where the concept of sharing commissions works. The salespeople know that they all benefit from every sale. This encourages cooperation and helping one another. A surprising result is that it does not encourage lack of productivity on the part of the lazy workers. In a small environment, it is very obvious after a short time who is not producing. That person has two choices, either to improve or to leave. Usually the less enthusiastic worker learns from the others and changes her or his behavior. This method becomes a better motivator for many salespeople since money is not the same trigger for everyone. With some adaptations, this reward system is effective in larger corporations and in other industries.

Rewarding loyalty in both customers and employees and rewarding cooperative rather than competitive behavior are just two methods of reinforcing trust within our business environments. There are no final answers; we are still searching for and trying new approaches. This is a time of change. This is a time when tension needs to be accepted as good because it forces creativity and a willingness to experiment. This is a time to treat employees and customers better.

Hiring people with character, training the new and current employees, insisting on accountability for actions, and rewarding loyal and productive employees and customers in new and creative ways are important steps. Combining these interdependent activities with the Exercises in Chapter 7 provides a framework for implementing trust within our places of work.

CONCLUSION

MEASURING THE TRUST FACTOR

Eight principles define trust: Compassion, Unity, Truthfulness, Fairness, Tolerance, Responsibility, Respect, and Service. These are the common principles taught by most religions and spiritual paths as mentioned in the Spirituality section of Chapter 6. These same principles define trust as it has been discussed throughout this book. They also define what I learned as I progressed through my adventures. The concepts are not new. As shown in my story, many of us just lost track of them as we found ourselves in a complex and confusing world. In order to maintain our grasp of these principles, we need to continually strive to keep simplicity in our lives and our jobs.

Exercise 7 sums up the notion of business trust in a two part activity. There are implications to our personal lives since the human element must be acknowledged in our workplace; but the focus is on business.

Part I of Exercise 7 assesses your personal trust factor. Part II of Exercise 7 uses the same approach to evaluate your organization. What is your trust factor? What is the trust factor of your company? Is there a compatibility? Honestly answer the questions in each Part with a yes or no, then follow the scoring directions at the end of Part II.

EXERCISE 7

WHAT IS YOUR TRUST FACTOR?

Part I—What is Your Individual Trust Factor?

1. Compassion
Do you care about and like yourself?
Do you care about the people you work with?

2. Unity
Do you believe that in working more closely with others, something better can be accomplished?
Are you willing to make a commitment to work more closely with others?

3. Truthfulness
Are you willing to be honest in your dealings with others?
Are you willing to be honest to yourself about your needs, wants and desires?
Are you willing to be honest with yourself about the integrity or lack of it at your company?

4. Fairness
Are you willing to treat employees and customers fairly?
Are you willing to insist on fair treatment for yourself?

5. Tolerance

Are you willing to accept the diversity of others?
Are you willing to allow others to have different views and opinions?

6. Responsibility

Are you willing to assume personal responsibility for your life?
Are you willing to assume your share of responsibility for the overall advancement of our society?

7. Respect

Are you willing to learn to respect others, their opinions and their beliefs?
Are you willing to respect yourself and what you do?
Are you willing to have respect for the earth and be conscious of not polluting the environment?

8. Service

Are you willing to help others at your company to advance and succeed?
Are you willing to commit to helping others in your community with time as well as money?

EXERCISE 7

WHAT IS YOUR TRUST FACTOR?

Part II—What is Your Company's Trust Factor?

1. Compassion

Does the company show that it cares about the individual workers?

2. Unity

Does the company encourage teamwork and cooperation?
Does the company reward cooperation or competition?

3. Truthfulness

Does the company provide honest information about its products or services to customers?
Is the company honest with its employees?

4. Fairness

Does the company treat its customers fairly?
Does the company treat its employees fairly?

5. Tolerance

Is the company tolerant of different views and new ideas?
Does the company encourage workers to be tolerant of coworkers?

6. Responsibility

Does the company promote personal responsibility by encouraging decentralization and allowing employees to make decisions?

Does the company allow employees to have a voice in company decisions?

Does the company encourage new ideas and new methods?

7. Respect

Does the company respect the opinions of its employees and customers?

Does the company respect the environment by not polluting?

8. Service

Does the company help employees to grow and advance within the firm?

Does the company encourage workers to contribute to the community?

Does the company offer company time to allow workers to help the community?

Scoring Your Individual Trust Factor and Your Company's Trust Factor:

>Score Part I and Part II separately.
>Assign one point for each "YES" answer.
>Add the number of points for Part I and Part II.
>Scores for Part I will range from 0-18.
>>Acceptable scores range from 10-18.
>Scores for Part II will range from 0-17.
>>Acceptable scores range from 10-17

If your score is in an acceptable range and your company is in an acceptable range, Congratulations! You and your company are role models and need to be encouraged to continue your quest.

If your score is not in an acceptable range, reconsider which principles you disagree with. How do these affect your view of trust and how others view you? Are you a trustworthy person? You might want to review the chapters in which the different principles are discussed:

>COMPASSION—Chapter 4
>UNITY—Chapters 1,5,2,8
>TRUTHFULNESS—Chapters 6,7,8
>FAIRNESS—Chapters 1,5
>TOLERANCE—Chapter 5
>RESPECT —Chapters 1,4,5
>RESPONSIBILITY—Chapters 1,5,7
>SERVICE—Chapters 3,7

If your score is in an acceptable range, but your company's score is not, consider what actions you can take to have your company change. If you feel there is little chance of improvement within your firm, what actions are you taking to find another job?

The challenge is for each of us to strive to become more compassionate, unified, truthful, fair, tolerant, respectful, responsible, and helpful to others. When we achieve these goals, we can trust in ourselves, trust in each other, and trust in a better world.

NOTES

[1] Peter F. Drucker, *Post-Capitalist Society* (New York: HarperBusiness, 1994), p.3.

[2] Alvin and Heidi Toffler, *Creating A New Civilization: The Politics of the Third Wave* (Atlanta: Turner Publishing, 1994), p.11.

[3] Drucker, p. 6.

[4] John Longworth, "American Dreams and Nightmares: Hanging Tough" (Albuquerque Journal, May 1994), p. 4B.

[5] Joel Swerdlow, "Information Revolution," *The National Geographic*, 188:4 (October 1995), p. 15.

[6] This continuum is presented as part of a new management model of the Academy of Management, a nonprofit organization in Cincinnati, Ohio that researches and teaches new management concepts.

[7] Lawrence M. Krauss, *Fear of Physics: A Guide for the Perplexed* (New York: Basic Books, a Division of Harper Collins Publisher, 1993), p. xi.

[8] Krauss, p. 25.

[9] Krauss, p. 25.

[10] Lloyd Motz and Jefferson Hane Weaver, *The Story of Physics* (New York: Avon Books, 1992), p. 122.

[11] Herbert Muschamp, "Architecture View: Buildings Born of Dreams and Demons," *The New York Times* (January 7, 1996), p. 27H.

[12] Motz and Weaver, p. 390.

[13] Krauss, p. 83.

[14] Motz and Weaver, p. 390.

[15] Sidney Lumet, "Why Reality Will Never Compute," *The New York Times* (January 14, 1996), p. 19H.

[16] Malcolm W. Browne, "A Quark Divided," *The New York Times* (January 14, 1996), p. 15.

[17] John L. Casti, *Complexification: Explaining a Paradoxical World Through the Science of Surprise* (New York: Harper Perenniel, 1995), p.14.

[18] David Parker and Ralph Stacey, *Chaos, Management and Economics: The Implications of Non-Linear Thinking* (London: Institute of Economic Affairs, 1994), p.11.

[19] Margaret J. Wheatley, *Leadership and the New Science: Learning About Organization from an Orderly Universe* (San Francisco: Berrett-Koehler, 1992), p. 96.

[20] John Flick, "Mind For All Matters," *Albuquerque Journal* (December 30, 1995), p. 2A.

[21] Casti, p. 41.

[22] Erich Fromm, *To Have or To Be?* (New York: Harper & Row Publishers, 1956). pp. 5-6.

[23] Fromm, p. 7.

[24] Fromm, p. 5.

[25] Robert X. Boyd, "Nurturing comes naturally," *Knight Ridder Newspapers*, reprinted in *Albuquerque Journal* (June 23, 1996), p. 1C.

[26] Robert A. Johnson, *WE: Understanding the Psychology of Romantic Love* (San Francisco: Harper & Row Publishers, 1983), p. 201.

[27] Erich Fromm, *The Art of Loving* (New York: Harper & Row Publishers, 1956), p. 60.

[28] Benjamin DeMott, "Sure, We're All Just One Big Happy Family," *The New York Times* (January 7, 1996), Section 2, p.1.

[29] Francis Mancini, "Media, Academia Undervalue Diverse Viewpoints," *Providence Journal-Bulletin*, reprinted in *Albuquerque Journal* (June 5, 1996), 13A.

[30] Alex Roland, "Large Craft Warnings," a book review of *No Downlink* by Claus Jensen and *The Challenger Launch Decision* by Diane Vaughan, *The New York Times Book Review* (January 28, 1996), p. 16.

[31] "An Open Letter to Governor Gary Johnson From 11 People Affected by Indian Gaming," *Albuquerque Journal* (August 13, 1995), p. 8B.

[32] This information is derived from material taught by the Academy of Management in Cincinnati, Ohio. The use of the information presented here is solely the interpretation of the author.

[33] This question and the following activity are variations of suggestions from an article by Philip Gerard, "Creating Discoveries for Creative NonFiction," *Writer's Digest* (February 1997), pp. 28-31.

[34] This activity is loosely derived from an assessment activity used by Words and Solutions, a business consulting firm in Albuquerque, New Mexico and based on technology developed by The Impact Group. The actual instrument is more complex and is part of a process for improving productivity. It is not used to assess individual strengths as interpreted by the author.

[35] This is an adaptation from a three-step process suggested by Peter F. Drucker in *Post Capitalist Society*, p. 160. His process discusses turning organizations around, not assessing individuals.

[36] Audibert Jones & Associates in Farmington, CT.

[37] Cheryl A. Chatfield (Chasser), "How Adolescents' Affective Responses to Four Short Stories Relate To The Factors of Age, Sex and Intelligence," Ph.D. Dissertation (Storrs, CT: University of Connecticut, 1976).

INDEX

THE NOTTINGHAM INSTITUTE

The Nottingham Institute is a nonprofit organization committed to education through training and publications in the area of entrepreneurship, communication, and leadership.

Seminars, based on this book, are available to corporations in the following areas:

Managers/Owners - How To:

- Encourage employee loyalty
- Improve communication
- Hire better workers
- Be better leaders
- Insist on accountability while providing more freedom
- Trust your employees
- Adapt to change

Employees - How To:

- Assume Personal Responsibility
- Effectively work in a 21st century business
- View yourself as an entrepreneur
- Feel more secure about your future
- Create your own future
- Work efficiently within a team
- Trust your employer

The Nottingham Institute also provides workshops for public and private school teachers and administrators in the areas of goal setting and trust.

The Nottingham Institute
4601 Montano NW No. 219
Albuquerque, New Mexico 87120
Phone: 505-899-5293
Email: NottInst@aol.com
FAX: 505-899-9452